BOOK I

HE'S JUST A MAN

MAKING THE MOST OF YOUR WOMANLY POWER

REBECCA WARNER

Book 1 - HE'S JUST A MAN   Making the Most of Your
Womanly Power

Copyright 2015 Rebecca Warner/Saisons D'Amour Publishing
www.rebeccajwarner.com

ISBN-10: 1516934563
ISBN-13: 978-1516934560

All incidents, dialogues and examples in this book are real.
Names have been changed to protect the not-so-innocent.

Cover Consultant: Johnny King Designs
www.johnnykingdesign.com

TESTIMONIALS ABOUT REBECCA WARNER

I've known Rebecca since 1980, when we were both in our early 20s and living in Miami. Even then, she had men figured out. She thinks like a man, but she is also one of the most "kick ass" feminine women I've ever known. She is a powerful combination of confidence and beauty, both inside and out. Rebecca is the authority on men and relationships, and I can say this with confidence because without her guidance, I would never have gotten my millionaire husband to the altar!

Brenda Lasker Gaines

I met Rebecca when we lived in Miami Lakes in the early 1980s. We found we really liked each other just as friends, and we became each other's sounding boards for relationships. She was always confident where men were concerned, and even dated several men at the same time. When I asked her if they knew about each other, she said, "If they ask, I tell them." I asked her how they felt about it, and she said, "If they don't like it, they know where the door is." I had never met a woman like her, and once I had a chance to ask a man she was dating what was so special about her. He pointed to the top of his head, then down at his feet as he said, "From the top of her head, to the tip of her toes." That said it all about Rebecca.

Joseph Langsam

I first met Rebecca when I was just newly married to my first husband. She was in her early 20s and I was amazed how she was able to walk into a room and took control in the most unobtrusive way. Her banking clients, male or female, hung onto every recommendation she would make. I know her book is about "men" but honestly she gained knowledge about human nature early on. Her advice is dead on and being head strong and afraid of my own shadow, I never listened. She helped me to appreciate all that I had to offer, slowly my confidence grew stronger and I knew that I could choose the man that I wanted... I did not have to settle. It would be my choice to have a man in my life or not .. I was good in my own skin and I knew I did not need a man. This left me open to endless possibilities... Lucky for the guy I married, an attorney, I chose him and he gets to spend his life in my loving arms happy to take care of all my needs... Thanks Rebecca for all the late night discussions your advice was priceless.

Julie Ruigomez-Patterson

Rebecca and I spent many hours together discussing men and relationships. I knew she had a great marriage to a successful and good-looking man who adored her. I learned that she had dated many men, loved more than one of them, and had several marriage proposals, so of course I wanted to learn what she knew. I always admired Sean Penn as a famous actor, and I knew we had one specific interest in common. After the devastating earthquake in Haiti in 2010, Sean Penn lent his time, his voice and his wallet to the effort to stabilize and rebuild. As a flight attendant, I was able to do my part in collecting literally tons of goods to take with me on my flights there. Among the many hats I wore, I also became an emissary for the Art Creation Foundation for Children in Jacmel, Haiti. One day, lo and behold, Sean Penn was in first class on my flight back from Haiti. I very much wanted to talk to him, but I hesitated for all the reasons you would imagine. But then I heard Rebecca's voice in my head saying, "He's just a man!" With that mantra bolstering me, I sat down across from him and we talked about our mutual interest and efforts in Haiti. I gave him my emissary business card; and even though I knew that I would never hear from him, I had done something I never would have done if not for Rebecca--I took a chance, and I was a better woman for it.

Sue Thomas

ABOUT WOMEN AND MEN...

I moved to Miami, Florida after graduating college in 1975, *when women were riding the crest of the wave that was the Sexual Revolution.* It was a period when women were able to explore their sexuality without fear or condemnation, thanks to the women's movement, which gave single women access to birth control. Did you know that until 1972, it was illegal for unmarried women to be prescribed birth control pills?

It was a wonderful time to be a single woman in her 20s! I had a fun and exciting single life and a financially rewarding career, with no need for a man to make my life better. It was already great! When I met my wonderful husband, I wanted to marry him; I did not need to marry him.

That is the kind of lifestyle many women like me enjoyed, because we had the freedom to establish a whole new base of power during that time...and we made the most of it.

And we talked about it—a lot. It was a time like none before when women were able to define and articulate their wants and needs in sex and relationships. We weren't going to settle for mediocre anything, especially sex!

We could concentrate on careers that wouldn't get derailed by an unintended pregnancy, take our time in finding the right man for us, and enjoy sex with multiple partners without fear of pregnancy or disease. This led to significantly greater independence for women.

Sexual freedom gave women power over their own lives. Women were no longer seen as the "property" of a man through marriage. (Think *Mad Men*.) Women could delay marriage and child bearing and pursue a career.

Having so much choice available to our generation was so liberating! Here is what you must understand about the many women who were an inspiration for this book: We saw a man, we wanted that man, we had sex with that man, we had sex with other men while having sex with that man, we didn't apologize for it, we embraced our sexuality, we demanded good sex and respect from a man, and we made men work for us, for our sex, for our love.

And all of that experience, all of those decades of talking and listening and acting and learning with dozens of women and men, are brought to you in Book 1: HE'S JUST A MAN, Making the Most of Your Womanly Power. Books 2 & 3 will discuss relationships and marriage.

In HE'S JUST A MAN, you will learn what we came to know: That women have what men want, and by learning to make the most of our womanly power, we could have *the man* whom we wanted.

Now it's your turn!

To My Husband, Jason
for loving me exactly as I am

WHAT I MEAN BY
"HE'S JUST A MAN"

There is a single and simple basic premise when it comes to understanding a man.

No matter how rich, how famous, how handsome, or how powerful he is, he is still *just* a man. As basically as it can be said, he operates from one place, and that one place is between his legs. He is such a simple creature in that respect, and regardless of what other trappings surround him, it all comes down to that.

Over the years, I have had many women talk to me about their issues with men. Somehow, they couldn't get that man to treat them as they wished to be treated, or to love them as they wished to be loved. As I listened, I was baffled that these women who had much to offer, who were successful in so many other areas of their lives, were at a loss when it came to how to be successful with men.

The song was always a familiar one—maybe different lyrics—but always the same tune: I can't get him to..., he won't..., he doesn't... he hasn't...

And I would look at the woman and say, "Really, what's the problem? He's *just* a man!" Then we talked about what that meant.

A man is not less than you nor greater than you. He is a man, and like all men since the beginning of time, he is in *pursuit* of a female. Once you understand and truly believe that concept—which you will after you read this book—you will have your love life under control.

This book will help you understand men. It will help you understand what makes a man want a woman, and it will help you achieve your goal in finding a man to share your life in a way that leaves you happy and fulfilled.

All you need to find a strong, loving man is the knowledge and understanding of the *power* you have as a woman. This book will guide you in *Making the Most of Your Womanly Power*.

Now you can enjoy learning how special and significant it is that you are a *woman*... because, after all, he's *just* a man.

CHAPTER ONE

MAKING THE MOST OF YOUR WOMANLY POWER

Power is a word that can have negative connotations, like power-mad, and power-hungry. But the dynamics of power simply means the capacity to have others do as you would like them to do.

When I began writing my column, *Miss Romantiquette: On the Etiquette of Romance*, for a local periodical, I began the series with a column based upon emails from a new friend who was having a difficult time with her long-term boyfriend. I changed the names, of course, but nothing else.

I got a call from the editor of the newspaper, telling me that a couple had just left his office after coming in and claiming that the column was about *them*. "Who is this Miss Romantiquette, and how did she know about us?" they demanded to know.

Here's the column:

Dear Miss Romantiquette,

My boyfriend of seven years, Jim, just broke up with me for the sixth time. Each time I am heartbroken, but I always take him back. I have always worked so hard to delight and please him. I see now that it has taken way too much of my energy, but I love being in a relationship. I have not been alone since I was sixteen. I have always adored being in a relationship and have had very long-term relationships. Even though I always felt I was walking on eggshells with Jim, it seemed to be worth it for the times that he was loving and treated me well and gave me nice presents, which I always thought was a way of showing me he loved me, even if he wasn't always good to me. But there were so many other times that he put me down and made me feel bad about myself. He was even jealous about my close relationship with my daughters, and put me between a rock and a hard place more than a few times when I had to choose between being with him or my daughters. I have been told many times that I am a good mother, and a good daughter to my parents, and a good friend, but obviously I'm not a good girlfriend!

I don't want to take him back again, because he has hurt me so much, but I love him and I'm afraid I'll give in. I am so tired of working so hard for his love, and I want it to be better this time around. What do you suggest?

Susan

Dear Susan,

Well, I suggest you take the time, this sixth time around, to consider some very important issues before you even contemplate taking Jim back.

First, it is good that you know that you are a good mother, good daughter, and good friend. This means you recognize that you have worth. Knowing this, you have a good place to start in building something you seem to be lacking--self-esteem, which is essential in any kind of romantic relationship.

There's an old saying, but it bears repeating here: "Before you can love someone else, you have to love yourself." When you love yourself, no one can make you feel bad about yourself, as Jim did. No one can put you down, and as Eleanor Roosevelt said, "No one can make you feel inferior without your consent." When a man finds it necessary to put you down, it is because of his insecurity, and no matter how much you try to please him, it will never be enough. Using all of your energy to please a man and expecting nothing in return will not earn you his respect, either; and respect is the bedrock of any successful relationship.

So before you seriously consider taking Jim back, work on the aspects of your life that are positive. Ask yourself what makes you a good mother, a good daughter, a good friend? You love the way you are in those relationships, and in return, you are loved and treated well. This will build your confidence. Then when any man tries to make you feel bad, you can look at him and honestly say, "I know I'm a good person, and I know I am loved by others because of that. If you can't treat me well and love me just as I am, you have no place in my life." And mean it!

Finally, ask yourself if Jim makes you happy more often that he makes you sad. If the answer is no, then why would you want to go back to him? Make your own happiness around your family and friends, and around your own interests. Despite the fact that you have been in long-term relationships since you were sixteen, you must now become a wiser woman and learn that you do not need a man. A man should only be in your life if he makes your life better... and by better I mean he makes you happy, and he makes you feel respected and appreciated. It is very powerful and freeing to know you don't need a man. When you come to truly know and believe that, you will be free to pursue a happy and healthy romantic relationship.

Susan has the power within her to make Jim do what *she*

wants. But somewhere in the relationship, she relinquished her power to him. Once she did that, he had total control over her life.

What was so amazing about this entire "how did she know about us?" scenario was that the same story was true for two sets of complete strangers — one of them a couple that I, of course, didn't even know.

That was an eye-opener for me, because even though I knew that the same dynamics have played out in relationships throughout history, here was one that hit really close to home. People go through the same things, the same kinds of power struggles emerge, relationships go through the same trials, love is stumped and thwarted and renewed and reinvigorated—and the same story, different era, different players, repeats itself.

What you are learning in this book is not groundbreaking, because whatever successful strategies women have incorporated to find a mate, are as old as time itself.

You have to look at men differently than you have in the past. You might assume that it is a man's playing field out there, but it isn't. It's *our* playing field, and if you think about it, we only assume it is a man's playing field because he asks us out. He shows interest in us and chooses us. Sure, this puts us at a disadvantage, but your normal man feels at a disadvantage, too.

Please realize that there are so many good men out there who are hoping to find someone to love, just as you are. You may need to make some serious adjustments to your attitude and your beliefs. Don't worry, it doesn't require a lot of work, just a bit of enlightenment and acceptance.

Just because someone is a "nice guy" does not mean he is a wimp. Are you only attracted to men who treat you badly? If the answer is yes, then here is the first adjustment you need to make: *Stop thinking of yourself as "not good enough."*

4

Here's a favorite quote of mine, by author and columnist Anna Quindlen: *"After all those years as a woman hearing 'not thin enough, not pretty enough, not smart enough, not this enough, not that enough,' almost overnight I woke up one morning and thought, 'I'm enough.'"*

Low self-esteem is the only reason a woman allows anyone man or woman to treat her badly. This book shows you how to build your self-esteem, because as long as you have low self-esteem, you will not be able to have a rewarding relationship. But in the meantime, for our purposes here, let's employ the old saying, *"Fake it 'til you make it."*

Don't feel so good about yourself? Appearance a problem? Not as romantically or professionally successful as others? Poor self-esteem is something many women struggle with, and it is a weakness. And if there is one thing a man really dislikes in a woman, it is weakness. Are you always comparing yourself to others? Stop it. Are you less attractive than you *could* be? Okay, make yourself more attractive for yourself. When you feel good about yourself, you stop comparing yourself to others, and you can spend that wasted time and energy in better ways.

♀

I want to tell women that you need to love yourself and make yourself a priority. It's only when you are happy yourself, can you make everyone else around you happy.
~ Bipasha Basu, Indian Actress

All right, let's get this first one out of the way. Want to look better? Eat less and move more. Exercise. (I heard that groan!) It doesn't matter if you hate it, there's a reason we hear and read about it everywhere exercise is nothing but beneficial. Even if you are perfectly fit, you can still benefit from exercise. And if you are not perfectly fit, then the need is obvious. Exercise gives you a feeling of doing something positive. You really sweated, and it feels great! Exercise relieves tension, sexual frustration, and bad moods. Endorphins, you know. And you start to feel in control of yourself, which feeds into so many other facets of your life. Finally, you are going to look better, so for your own sake, get out of the pillows and go for a walk, go to a gym, or take a dance class. *Just move!*

And the term "acceptance" needs to be a larger part of everyone's vocabulary. Some things in life simply *are*. Are your thighs too large, and no amount of exercise or dieting renders them slim? Learn to accept that. What you look like does count, but it counts for reasons that most people overlook. What you look like shows others how *you* feel about *you*, and about your willingness to do what it takes to improve your appearance, while accepting the imperfections you were born with.

It's about caring for you. Caring for yourself has the happy side effect of impacting the people in your life positively. It's a win/win. Work with what you have to make it the best it can be.

But, are you just too damn lazy to make any changes? Then you just might find yourself alone, because if you can't change, can't grow, and can't set and achieve goals, what makes you think you *deserve* a man's admiration, much less his respect? So what if you are fifty pounds overweight? Get active, shed ten pounds, and you will feel better about yourself. And when you feel better about yourself, that is reflected in everything that happens around you. If you just can't shed that weight, make the most of your appearance.

No matter what face and body you are given, you are still a woman, and there is such power in that simple reality.

A dear friend of mine is an obstetrician and gynecologist.

He sees thousands of women each year, and they come in all shapes and sizes, in all degrees of attractiveness. Here's the breakdown, according to him: There are beautiful women who have no lovers nor any boyfriends, and with many, that situation doesn't change much from year to year. Then there are some very unattractive women who have adoring husbands and boyfriends, who are very happy with themselves and their lives.

My favorite story of his involved a delivery of a baby for a woman who—to quote him—"was the largest woman I had ever seen." Shortly after the delivery, a nasty scene ensued in the waiting area that involved her husband and her boyfriend. Apparently there was a dispute about whose baby it was and who loved that woman more. Sure, this is fodder for *Jerry Springer*, but it is real life, and there is a point here: A huge woman, not necessarily attractive by society's standards, had two men fighting over her. I have no doubt as to why. It is because she is a woman who knows how to make men love her. And it has nothing to do with looks, obviously, so you can't use that excuse.

How many times have you seen women who are, by society's standards, unattractive, yet they have a loving man in their lives? You have asked yourself, "What does she have that I don't?"

It's natural to wonder about that, and to compare yourself to her. But your comparison addresses only physical attributes, at least initially.

What is most important, what you need to be thinking about instead, is how to love yourself, which you'll learn in Chapter Three.

Now let's look at how men have usurped our womanly power, and how we get it back!

CHAPTER TWO

ÍN THE BEGÍNNÍNG...

Adaption from the writing of Matthew Henry

<u>The Woman</u>
If man is the head, she is the crown
Man was dust refined, but the woman was double refined,
Once removed further from the earth.
Woman was made from Adam's rib;
Not from his head to rule over him,
Nor from his feet to be trampled upon by him,
But out of his side to be equal to him,
From under his arm to be protected by him,
And near to his heart to be loved by him.

A man's desire for a woman is as old as Adam and Eve. The story as written in the Bible, however, did not do women any favors. It was Eve who ate the forbidden fruit. She *seduced* Adam into doing the same. She had the power to do that. Therefore, according to man's written account of this incident, it is woman's fault that the world was cast into sin.

And men have been afraid of women ever since.

Even today, "religious leaders" preach men's fear of women. Pat Robertson, former Southern Baptist minister and Chairman of the Christian Broadcasting Network is quoted as saying:

"Feminism is a socialist, anti-family political movement that encourages women to leave their husbands, kill their children, practice witchcraft, destroy capitalism, and become lesbians."

Now here's the real definition of feminism: The advocacy of women's rights on the grounds of political, social, and economic equality to men.

Men are afraid for women to find equality in those areas, because they know women already have an awesome amount of power by simply being a woman. We hold their egos in the palm of our hands, and we can crush them with a disapproving look, a subtle snub, or a disparaging remark; and men intuitively know that.

In ancient Egypt, which knew nothing about the Garden of Eden, women held positions of power equal to men. There were always goddesses as well as gods. Women were natural rulers, and enjoyed sex as much as men, without condemnation.

As the world changed, women were cast into subservient roles and kept under a man's control. In Jesus' time (I promise this is not a religious book, but so much of our *predicament* is tied to interpretations of the Bible), Jewish wives were forbidden to leave their homes without covering themselves from head to foot. They were not allowed to look at or speak to another man. If there were even a hint of compromise, a doubt in the husband's mind about his wife's "fidelity," he could divorce her that very day. Many women were so afraid of this fate that they would not leave their homes. And why did Jewish law keep women so enslaved?

Because it was believed that if a man got even a glimpse of any tiny part of a woman's body, then *she might tempt him.*

Try to understand the importance of that. Men subjugated women, made them virtual prisoners in their homes for fear that another man might be tempted by her—*and that would be her fault.* Funny how some things just do not change. If a man rapes a woman today, well it was her fault for wearing that short skirt and tempting him.

Think how often you have heard this nonsense. A man turns violent, and it's the *woman's fault.*

Now let's make a connection here and turn this around. What this comes down to is this: Man is rendered weak because he wants our sex. Throughout history, man's weakness was his weapon. An unfaithful woman was executed immediately   no questions asked. A man, on the other hand, could find any excuse and without answering to a single soul, he could divorce his wife and take another all in the same day—literally—and suffer no consequences.

So throughout history, and up through today, a weak man can have fifteen lovers a month, and he's a stud. A strong woman can have fifteen lovers in her lifetime, and she's a slut. There's a double standard practically built into our societies and our psyches that inhibits women from being as powerful as they can be. Women who would dare to enjoy sex with a number of different partners are denigrated by men, while men are free to enjoy sex with as many women as they want without reprisal or consequence.

And if you let that kind of absurdity guide your life, then you will find it much more difficult to come into your full power as a woman.

♀

Moving into the 21st century, let's look to the modern *Urban Dictionary* to get men's updated take on women.

(Women are) *highly attracted to males of the species who*

are reasonable to look at, have jobs, are relatively kind, sometimes take out trash, and treat them like equals (not superiors, not inferiors -- equals.) Happily give blowjobs(sic) *in return.* (We'll cover this last assumption later in the book.)

To those men who cannot procure them (because said men are too mean, stupid, sexist, ugly, and unaccomplished) they (women) *cause intense feelings of failure, hatred, prejudice, violence, and* (the) *need to post on boards stereotyping all women with one narrow, negative definition. Said men then jack off alone.*

When said beings (women) *reject such specimens of men or express an intelligent opinion, they are bitches.*

When they don't put out, they are also bitches. When they do, they are sluts.

Of course this is tongue-in-cheek, but the last line of this is indeed the way society thinks, and that way of thinking has to stop—and stopping it starts with *you.*

Stopping it starts with you and every other woman who refuses to accept this stereotyping simply because she chooses to have sex simply for her own pleasure. This book is intended to change your way of thinking. It is meant to change the way you look at yourself. And most of all, it is meant to change the way you look at men.

Remember this as you go forward—the male pursues the female. He goes after *it, the essence of what makes us a woman.* It has been thus in the animal kingdom (of which we are a part) from the beginning of time. It stems from biological roots and behavioral memories that are deep and ancient. Females are given certain biological aids, which cause a male to want to *act* to have her sexually.

♀

Nature makes woman to be won, and men to win.

George William Curtis
(American writer and public speaker 1824 1892)

Civilization has made it necessary for the male of the human species of the animal kingdom to take controlled steps as he acts (takes action) to get from a woman what he is engineered—physically and psychologically—to have. Her sex. He wants it, you have it. Fortunately, we as women were built with the same physical and psychological needs, but we have to go about meeting those needs in a different way than men. It's a ritual however, as old as time—we *mate.*

Taken in its most base context, the animal kingdom mates to propagate. We reproduce, thus ensuring the survival of our species. All animals have pheromones, though not until 1986 did Dr. Winnifred Cutler, Athena Institute's founder and President, prove their existence in humans.

Pheromones are naturally-occurring chemical substances the body excretes externally, conveying information to and triggering responses from others from within the same species. For example, female dogs in heat emit pheromones that attract male dogs. Women and men excrete pheromones, which breaks this whole sexual process down to "chemical attraction" between sexes. You might say that exposure to pheromones is the essence of sex.

It really is that basic. We were meant to mate, to procreate, and to propagate the species. This is what drives us to have sex.

Society, religion and laws have muddied these clear waters. But let's get back to where we started... the basics. Men want what we have. We have the power to control them because of that. Does that sound ridiculous? Too simple? Well, it's not, because after all, he's *just* a man.

CHAPTER THREE

LOVING YOURSELF: BUILDING YOUR SELF ESTEEM

The strongest factor for success is self-esteem: Believing you can do it, believing you deserve it, believing you will get it.

You have to scrape off years of muck that has stuck to your psyche, and ask yourself this question: If I *never* find a man to love, what is the worst that can happen?

The worst that can happen is that you are alone.

Are you alone now? If so, do you still breathe, blink, eat, laugh, sigh, pee, smell, hear, and talk? Of course you do. Now does having a man in your life change those things? No, of course not. Your very life, your very being, your ability to draw a breath and awaken every morning *does not depend on a man.*

Simply stated, you don't need a man to live.

But, you might say, I need a man to live *happily.* No, you don't. You may *want* a man to make you happier, but you don't *need* a man to live or to be happy. Learn to believe this in your heart, to know it for a fact, and when you do, you will find a peace and happiness that no man can give you. And when—as a woman who is happy and loves herself—you do find a good man, you will have the primary ingredient for a great relationship.

Every day you lament about being alone, and every bit of energy you waste feeling sorry for yourself, robs you of your right to be happy. To be happy, you need to feel good about yourself. So let's work on self-esteem.

Self esteem is dependent on your self-approval, not a man's approval of you.

One of the best ways to build your self-esteem is to like yourself. This is very important because you have to answer some pretty tough questions down deep in your soul to get there.

Let's start with this one: If you stepped through a magic door into your future, and you learned that you would never have a man to love and no man to love you *ever*, and this was set in stone and could not be changed, how would you approach your life differently?

If you knew your happiness depended solely on you, and not on some man coming to save you from singledom, would you choose a different way to live your life? After all, it is *your life*. And life is what we make of it.

Give this question some thought: Would you take your waiting self down from the shelf and travel? Would you learn to play the piano? Would you get involved in volunteer activities? What would you do to enrich your life, knowing a man will not be doing that for you?

Steps to Becoming a Confident, Independent Woman

One of the most difficult things women face is being lonely. I once read that a sign of good mental health is being able to be alone and not be lonely. That is not by any means the sole definition of good mental health, but it works with other parts of your life to give you a completely healthy outlook on life. There is nothing wrong with being alone and there is no shame in it. It's a good place to start. If you have no one but yourself for companionship, then learn to be your own best friend.

Before you become your own best friend, you have to like

yourself. Does that sound nuts? Well, think about it. You make friends with people you like. You become best friends with the people you like most.

So, as is true for a relationship with a man, you have to like before you love. If you don't like yourself—if you put yourself down every time you look in the mirror, if you think you're stupid, if you don't like your lack of ambition or your bad habits—then how can you be your own best friend? You start by liking the person you see in the mirror each day.

Looks Matter...
(but not like you think they do)

I am going to begin with what may seem the shallowest issue— your appearance. But until you can look in the mirror and not only accept, but *like* what you see, you won't have a chance at becoming self confident and, consequently, loving yourself.

Remember the overweight woman who had two men fighting over her. Somewhere along the line, she became comfortable in her own skin and decided to embrace her womanliness. When you acknowledge that you are the best you are going to be (that is, after you have put effort into getting there) and you first come *to accept* that, you are on the road to self confidence. The next step after acceptance is *to like* who you are. When you find out you are a likable person, you can then work on other attributes—such as your personality, your sincerity, your knowledge, your spiritual awareness—and then you will come *to love* yourself. Accept —> Like —> Love...

There are steps you can take to accomplish this. Use the times you are alone to find out who you are. Acknowledge your pain and loneliness. Are you lonely because there is no one else just to talk to? And why is that? Have you developed any interests that help you be around people? Ask yourself, "What really interests me?"

For example, are you interested in cleaning up the environment? Call an ecological society and find out about groups in your area that are active, and then show up at one of those activities. Do you have an interest in learning about anything in particular? Get online and find groups that are involved in what interests you, and join up. Love animals? Get in touch with your local Humane Society to find out how you can volunteer or become involved in fund-raising, which leads to group activities and new contacts.

If you let your shyness, lack of confidence, or apathy hold you back from *mingling*, then you won't even get to the point of making new friends or meeting a man—let alone taming him. Hold up your head, smile, make eye contact, and learn to converse (next chapter). You can do it! Each time you do, you gain more confidence and become naturally sociable. So again, *fake it 'til you make it*. Act the part of a confident, interested and interesting person, and you will become that person. It happens quite naturally, as you will soon learn.

Easy Steps to Improving Your Personality

Does the thought of showing up alone and joining a group of strangers scare you? It scares most people. So be prepared. One of the biggest favors you can do for yourself is to become knowledgeable. It is such a simple thing to do; it just requires some suspension of laziness. Read. Get on the Internet and explore. Watch programs that relate to your interests, and even those that don't.

The most important thing you can do is *listen and ask questions of other people.* In other words, take an interest in other people, and you will become a more interesting person yourself. You have some knowledge, but you can always acquire more. The greatest way to become part of a group—whether it's you and one other person, or you in a crowd—is to *listen and ask questions.*

"Half of seeming clever is keeping your mouth shut at the right times."

~ Patrick Rothfuss, Author

There is an art to that, and if you learn this one simple thing, you will see a big difference in your life. When I say ask questions, this is what I mean: Let's say someone at that enviro-cleanup get-together starts talking about something you don't know about or understand. How many times have you been listening to someone talk and not had a clue what he or she is saying? Yet you either keep your mouth shut or wait until you can jump in with a sentence that begins with, "I." Come on, be honest. You absolutely must learn to be an active listener—active with your brain, not your mouth. When you don't know something, or someone says something of interest that you would like to know more about, that is the time to open your mouth. *Ask.*

There are many ways to ask a question, but it should be pertinent and it should be sincere. If you listen, really listen to someone, without waiting for that breathless moment when you can jump in with your own comment, you will learn much and you will be liked more. And when that someone you are listening to says something about which you think, *What is he talking about?* don't stop with that thought. Ask what he's talking about, and then listen again.

Let's do some scenarios. You are with another person, or you are in a group of people.

Man talking: I read a book about Leonardo da Vinci's life and it was fascinating.

You could care less about Leonardo da Vinci, other than knowing he painted the *Mona Lisa,* but that doesn't matter. You might not care to learn anymore about da Vinci, either. That's fine. But you can use this opportunity to learn about the person you are listening to.

You: What made it fascinating?

Him: Learning about all the things he invented.

You: Really? What things did he invent?

Him: Well, like landing gear.

You: Landing gear? Like on a plane?

Him: More like a helicopter.

You: And what year was this?

Him: Early sixteenth century.

You: Incredible! What else did he invent?

See? You didn't know a thing, but you certainly don't sound stupid. You are learning…and you are giving him an opportunity to talk and to share knowledge. He will like that about you. You will like that about yourself. Where's the flaw in that?

Now what you may have learned about this person is that he is egotistical and just loves to hear himself talk, which will be indicated by whether he dismisses you and your questions; or that he is an open, modest person who is happy to share and converse.

You then know whether or not to pursue the conversation...and him.

And *smile* when it is appropriate. Smiling denotes a good attitude, confidence, and pleasure. Nod your head, look into his eyes. He will be flattered. I am using the "he" pronoun, but it is imperative that you become a good listener to both sexes. You have nothing to lose with a woman, you're not courting her. So practice listening and asking questions at *any given opportunity.*

Notice that what you have done in these instances is you have taken a small context of what that person said and incorporated it into questions that *do not show your ignorance.* On the contrary, your curiosity shows your intelligence in having listened and taken an interest in learning. If you are interested in da Vinci, by all means ask about that. Either way, you have entered into intelligent conversation *that doesn't revolve around you.*

Your turn may come, but even if it doesn't, you are better off because you have shown interest in another person, making that person feel better about himself or herself, and you have learned something. And therefore, you have become a more interesting person. It is a very positive thing to listen, ask, and learn. Only good comes of it, and the very best part of listening is that people end up thinking you are a brilliant conversationalist. Even if you didn't ask a question, but only *listened,* and I do mean attentively and openly, with your eyes and ears totally devoted to what is being said, you will still be perceived as a good conversationalist. And a nice person. And a person someone wants to be around. Listening is *hearing.* It is "lending your ear," to someone, and that is a generous and coveted trait.

Now, suppose you do have specific knowledge of da Vinci. That's okay—show it off. But there is an art to doing that, as well. While someone is speaking, listen for an opportunity to insert your knowledge. This may take the conversation in another direction, but that's okay because it's pertinent.

There is another side to this coin of conversation. If you are smart, if you are knowledgeable, if you are conversant on many subjects, don't be afraid to show it. Don't hijack a conversation to show off your knowledge, but contribute as you can, with the confidence that you will be heard for what you are—smart and informed.

I have had some women tell me that if they let a man know how smart she is, it is a turn-off. How ridiculous. **If a man isn't man enough** to appreciate your intelligence, if he is not secure enough in himself to allow for your exhibition of knowledge, then he is not worth a single moment of your time.

With knowledge comes confidence. The more confident you are, the more you like yourself. Wherever you've picked up your knowledge, whether it's through education or everyday life lessons, you've learned and retained information for a reason, and that reason is that the knowledge has importance to you either personally or by how it affects the world around you.

Maybe you do have knowledge of da Vinci's inventions. Don't hide that knowledge, incorporate it into the conversation.

Here's an alternate scenario in the da Vinci discussion:

You: I've wanted to read that book because I've always had an interest in da Vinci as an inventor.

Him: Did you know he invented landing gear?

You: I did read that. Landing gear that would be more specific to a helicopter than an airplane though, right?

Him: That's right! He also invented scuba gear.

You: When he was living in Venice around 1500, yes. He designed his scuba gear for sneak attacks on enemy ships from underwater.

Him: Pretty incredible when you consider how long ago that was.

Now look at the higher level of communication that has been attained. You've engaged in conversation that clearly indicates you have much more to talk about.

This is why it pays to be learned, to read every chance you

get, and to listen as others talk so that you can obtain interesting information for future conversations.

Of course, there are other ways this can play out. If he says, "How does a girl know so much about inventions?" *You Are Out of There*. Why? Because he doesn't think women are equal to men in intelligence; and if he doesn't think a woman can be as intelligent as a man, then he doesn't think women are as good as men in any capacity. That's a sign of insecurity in a man, and it will translate into his treating you badly and putting you down to keep you in your place. That is not the type of man you want in your life, because he will only make you feel bad about yourself.

If he says, "Hey, I really don't know that much, I just heard some guys talking about da Vinci and the helicopter," then you have to make a decision about whether he is interesting enough to want to know more about him. This is when you try another subject, based on something else you have observed about him.

You will be able to tell pretty quickly if he is limited in knowledge himself, and is unable or unwilling to go any further in talking about anything that might be of interest to you. If he goes into the Marlins' dismal baseball season, and you don't know or care about baseball, you can listen politely and ask a question. But if you still have no interest in what he is saying about baseball, try to shift the subject to finding common ground—tastes in music, hobbies, or profession.

Remember, it's not just about you coming across as well-versed on a number of subjects, it's also about *his* intellect and ability to converse. If he can't interest you in the first round of conversation, chances are he never will. If you can't find any common ground, it won't get any better when you try to make a go of a relationship.

♀

Here's a hard one. You see a man who interests you, and he isn't with another woman. You'd like to meet him. What do you do?

One woman in her mid-twenties told me that she had no problem approaching a man to start a conversation. She said it can be something as simple as, "So, you like Jack and Coke?" Simple—basic even—but it is something. And the important thing is, she attempted to initiate a conversation.

Take control of your social life by getting over your apprehension in approaching a man. Sometimes men don't see you, or they're a bit shy themselves. So make him see you, or help him get past his shyness. You have absolutely nothing to lose. After all, he wasn't in your life ten minutes ago, so if that doesn't change after you've approached him, you haven't lost a thing. But you've *gained experience*, and every ounce of experience counts in this quest you are on.

If you have no experience doing this, due to lack of courage, that's okay. Just start. Do it. Practice. You may feel you have failed if he shows no interest in you, but you most certainly have not failed. You have succeeded in taking a step toward personal growth (because you moved out of your place of fear and attempted something new), plus you gained knowledge and experience. Each and every time you *try*, you experience success in some form or another—achievement of your goal (he is interested) or achievement of learning more about what works and doesn't work with certain approaches and actions.

You'll learn to increase your odds in making a connection in Chapter Six, where I talk about the art of flirting.

Another thing you can do that will help you feel better about yourself, and make others feel good about you, is to offer sincere compliments.

Have you ever been talking to someone, man or woman,

and thought to yourself, *Nice jacket*, or *Pretty eyes*, or *Those shoes are beautiful, I wonder where she got them*? but you didn't say anything to that person—you just left it as a thought? Speak up!

First rule: If you pay a compliment, make it sincere. If you have a positive, complimentary thought, then it is real, and worthy of being passed on. Never, ever make up something. It will come across as phony, because it is. But when you do have that nice thought, *open your mouth and let it come out.* Complimenting someone else does not detract from you. It enhances you and shows you are confident enough about yourself to share a good opinion, a kind thought. And again, it makes you more likeable.

Where a man is concerned, this is extremely important also. To become more attractive to a man, no matter what your physical attributes, you need to show some interest in him. How many times have you grabbed the conversational limelight with a man by giving him your life story on the first date, or even upon first meeting him? Do you really think anyone cares enough about anyone else to want to learn that person's entire personal history during the first real conversation? *Can it!* It is important to let him get to know you in his own way, at his own pace. Don't cram your life down his throat.

Actually, stop talking so much in general. Men intensely dislike women who cannot stop talking. I had a male friend who was going out with a hot, beautiful woman. He really wanted something to happen between them, but he simply could not stand being around her for any length of time because she never stopped talking. Incessant talking is a sign of insecurity, and nothing is more boring to a man than a woman who prattles on about everything from the woman at work she can't stand to the most recent antics of her cat. You've probably had girlfriends like this, and you have found them annoying enough to start avoiding them. Why wouldn't men do the same?

Here is a rule of thumb that is true for both sides of the conversation. If you have something to say, try to say it in thirty seconds. Then stop, and wait for him to say something. If he doesn't say anything, you can assume he's not particularly interested in what you're saying.

Time to stop talking about yourself or your interests or your point of view, and ask him a question, allowing him time to talk. Is he still talking two minutes later? No matter how smart a person is, if he dominates a conversation, he will be boring and even tiring to the other person.

While it's obvious when someone else talks a lot, it's not nearly as easy to evaluate your own conversational habits. Ask your friends whether they think you talk too much or interrupt their conversation or otherwise dominate your interactions. Insist that they be honest and not tell you what you want to hear, but instead, tell you how you really converse.

Have you ever had a conversation with a man who has talked of nothing but himself, asking you no questions about yourself, ignoring anything you have said, running right over your comment as if you never said it? Well, didn't you go away thinking he was selfish and *boring*? So what makes you think that same action on your part might be attractive to a man? Learn to *converse*. Conversation is give and take. Remember, asking questions and giving compliments are definite winning attributes. Some people listen with the goal of understanding what is being said. Some people listen with the goal of replying.

Be the person who listens not only to understand, but to learn.

When you are meeting a man for the first time, show an interest in him through your questions and compliments—again, they must be sincere. It's okay to ask, "What kind of work do you do?" Then to follow up with a polite question—any question—related to his response. Whatever he does, from ditch digger to CEO, he has something to tell you about his job. Don't forget the important Ws in asking questions—Who, What, Where, When, and Why. Incorporate any of those into a follow-up question, and you'll start the ball rolling. If you are thinking, *Gee, he sounds intelligent*, tell him. But remember, only pay him a compliment if you are honestly thinking something complimentary.

Now, here's a warning. If he just can't stop talking about himself, and really shows no interest in getting to know anything about you—get out of there. I mean it. He is a selfish person who is not worthy of your time. It doesn't matter if he's good looking and sexy as hell. If he doesn't care about you, doesn't care to know more about you, he is a loser. (More later on loser traits to beware of.)

One exception here. If you just want to have sex with him, put up with his narcissistic behavior and go for it. Just know that with selfish men, however, sex is never as good as it should be. But what the heck—you want him sexually and don't care if he never calls again.

Wait a minute, you might be thinking—*that's what men do, those jerks.* Ah, now you're getting the idea. Why shouldn't women be able to seduce men and walk away with no problem when men do just that all the time? I'll get into "thinking like a man" in a later chapter. I just wanted to note an *exception* to ditching a boring man.

Through questions and compliments, you are a more interesting, more likeable person. As you see people react positively to this behavior, your self-esteem will grow. You will feel good about yourself because you are "lending an ear," and giving others an opportunity to talk through answering your questions. And you'll feel good about yourself when you give someone else a compliment. If you haven't tried this, it may not sound realistic to you—how can I feel better about myself by telling someone else he/she looks good? Believe me, you will. Practice this, use it, get better at it. That is another example of "fake it 'til you make it." Do not be fake about your interest or compliments, but "fake" the ability to do these things well and with grace until it does become completely natural. Like anything new, it just takes practice.

Finally, *laugh*, honestly and fully, when he says something funny. Don't force it, but if it comes naturally, laughter is one of the most flattering things you can do for a person. Holding back on laughter for the purpose of looking sophisticated just makes you look dimwitted or cold-blooded.

You can do these, and other things, to become more popular. This isn't high school, this is real life and real stakes, and popularity matters in your adult life much more than it did in your younger years.

Count Your Blessings

Wait...What? What does gratitude have to do with personality? Think about it. If you count your blessings, you are a happier person. If you count your blessings *everyday* you will start feeling happier and more optimistic. Gratitude can take on a variety of forms.

Whether thankfulness manifests in an appreciation of the people in your life, feeling grateful for what you already have, living in the moment, or invoking frequent feelings of awe about the wondrousness of life, keeping a positive spin on things gives you a "high."

Scientists from the Center for Neuroeconomics Studies at Claremont Graduate University appear to have uncovered the hormone that makes us feel euphoric when we're feeling blessed: *oxytocin,* a powerful body chemical that's also activated during sex and breastfeeding.

A happier you means a less-defensive you, a less-troubled you, a less-critical you. It means the happiness you carry inside you is projected to the outside world, and it inevitably makes you a more pleasing person to be with.

"Joy is what happens to us when we allow ourselves to recognize how good things really are."

~ Marianne Williams

CHAPTER FOUR

CLASS

There is no way around the discussion of class if you want to be a woman who makes the most of her womanly power.

Class is one of those words that carries weight and intimidates. I wish there were another word for the same concept. Class is used so often that it is almost a cliché, but clichés are based on truth.

Being gracious is part of having class. Did you know that being gracious makes it much easier to make new friends of both sexes? Being polite is the basis of gracious, and just by saying "thank you" to someone new who has helped you, you are more likely to develop a friendship with that person.

Class is something everyone thinks they have, but that's just not possible, is it? Not everyone has a keen mind, a sense of humor, good taste, or class. But most of these traits can be developed or enhanced.

Men want to date and have relationships with a classy woman. Just take a look at most of the men's dating profiles on a dating site, and you will see that a number of them want to meet and date a woman who has "class." You are the one to decide if you want to develop society's definition of class. Or if you want to be even classier than you already are.

Individuality may be more important to you. If you choose to have green hair, tattoos, and multiple body piercings, or wear clothes that show off (versus accentuate) your hot body, do so!

Just accept that by virtually any standards, you are not projecting class.

But what *does* project class? Class is how you act, how you carry yourself, how you express yourself, and how you live your life. Women who don't have class are certainly able to develop that quality. Do you want to do this? Recognize that you have to really want it, and that it takes a strong willingness to make changes.

Start by reflecting on your own self, recognizing those qualities that you are missing, or recognizing those qualities that you already have, but could improve upon. Once you recognize these things, you can start working to build that attractive flair of class and sophistication.

♀

The Characteristics of Class

Back to "get smart." There is no doubt about it: *Perceived* class has little weight and value if the person behind it has no interesting thoughts, views, or observations. Being a classy woman requires the ability to share and challenge ideas and to be engaging company. You don't have to be argumentative or try to prove that you are right all the time, but you do have to possess a degree of wit and enjoy playful banter—*an integral part of flirting and intellectual foreplay.*

A classy woman embraces her femininity. Being a classy woman means having feminine demeanor and manners. In my opinion, this is one of the most important aspects of class— being gracious and polite. Femininity is really a woman's greatest strength. You don't need to best a man, you've already bested him just by being a woman, simply because you have

29

what he wants. A classy woman is a confident woman, one who showcases her womanliness in everything she does and every move she makes.

Men love the feminine things a woman does, from tilting her head to adjust her earring to emitting a clear, melodious, and happy laugh. Such a woman enjoys men and the reaction she gets from them, and she knows that the mental, physical, and sexual differences in her and a man are exactly as nature intended.

A sense of fashion is an essential part of class. Being a classy woman means having authentic style. While having an eclectic style may be considered cool, if you want to come across as a classy dresser, you can hardly go wrong with a business casual look or simple, clean cut, fitted (but not too fitted) attire. Simple colors like beige, white, and black flatter most women, and can be easily and attractively accessorized. Following temporary shock-value fashion trends and fads certainly does not add to being classy. This doesn't mean that you have to look boring or that you always have to blend in, but it does mean that you should not look like someone who is dying for attention. Know your body type well enough to clothe yourself in flattering fashions. Observe other women who have your body type and who look good in their clothes. Go to a store and ask a salesperson to make suggestions. Take your age and body type into account with each purchase you make.

"Dress shabbily, and they remember the dress. Dress impeccably, and they remember the woman."
~ *Coco Chanel*

A classy woman is elegant. Elegance is the top rung of

classy. The standard definition of elegance is: *Pleasingly graceful and stylish in appearance or manner*. People know elegance when they see it, although it is a difficult concept to specifically define.

One of the most attractive things you can do for your overall image is to learn to walk with purpose and grace. Develop a confident, heads-up, smooth gait. It gets noticed, and it says to men, *That's a confident woman*. Men find confidence very sexy —a definite turn-on.

How a woman carries herself is crucial. By "carries herself," I mean how she puts one foot in front of the other. You don't have to be a runway model who crosses one foot in front of the other as you sidle down the sidewalk. You just need to put one foot in front of the other without hobbling, stumbling, clunking, or jostling from side to side. If you hold your stomach in—and this is something you should learn to do as easily as breathing—your body automatically takes on a more elegant posture. It lifts the midsection of your body, and makes you feel as if you want to hold your shoulders up, not slouched.

Anyone can have good posture. Bad posture and a lumbering gait are nothing more than bad habits. Getting from point A to point B should not be a stalking walk propelled by hunched shoulders; rather, it should be a pleasant journey taken with confidence and style. As much time as we spend hunched over our computers these days, we can very easily develop a rounded back. So be aware of this, and perhaps try some yoga stretches to offset those effects.

I would like to give you some examples of some of the most elegant women the world has ever known. If you don't know who these women are, please Google them, and check out YouTube to see them in action. They exude femininity, charm, grace, and confidence.

Audrey Hepburn, an actress from "way back when," was perhaps the most elegant woman ever to appear on a movie screen. Her understated little black dresses, single strand of pearls, simply-coiffed hairstyle, and most of all, the way she carried herself, all gave her the essence of grace and class.

Marilyn Monroe was an unconventional and controversial combination of sexuality and class. She wasn't raised in a classy environment, but she was certain enough of her looks, smart enough in her thinking, and confident enough in her sexuality—knowing that men desired her—that she could be ultra womanly and feminine and sexy without apology. Because of the roles she played, Marilyn Monroe was often labeled a "dumb blonde," and less-than-classy, but in real life she was far from dumb. She was well read and could converse intelligently, and she embraced her femininity.

Grace Kelly, another actress from the 1950s and 1960s, was described as a "cool, crisp, classy, and collected blonde." She had the advantage of being born into an affluent family, and was so thoroughly enchanting that she became a real princess when she married the Prince of Monaco!

Jacqueline Kennedy Onassis was so elegant that she changed the style direction of a nation.

Princess Diana carried herself well, spoke softly, and learned as much as she could so that she could converse intelligently. Diana wore subtle but stylish clothes, exhibited her impeccable grooming, exuded femininity and elegance, and demonstrated her comfort in being with people from all classes. Her graciousness to all made her the very definition of class.

And Princess Kate, the current Princess of Wales, is carrying on every tradition of class that her deceased mother-in-law, Princess Diana, possessed.

Kate Middleton is the most elegant, gracious, beautiful

woman of our time. In the cases of Princesses Diana and Kate, neither woman was born into royalty, and because of that, both are referred to as a "the people's princess." Yet each of them is a perfect example of being able to make herself into a woman worthy of representing royalty.

Perhaps the most distinguishing character trait of both Diana and Kate was/is the ability to "walk with kings and talk with peasants, and treat them both the same." That ability is born from an inherent kindness. No one with class looks down on others simply because they are poor or uneducated. Everyone should be treated with dignity, unless and until they prove to be unworthy of such consideration.

In the entertainment arena, I admire Gwen Stefani's refinement and taste. She is always perfectly coiffed and impeccably dressed. She stands straight and tall and walks with grace and elegance, and she has a smile that is welcoming while her banter is intellectually engaging.

Scarlett Johansson is a movie star for whom class is a constant companion.

Beyoncé is a modern-day example of the kind of class/sexuality combination that Marilyn Monroe possessed. A woman who exudes a combination of sexuality and class inevitably rises above the crowd. Add to that her intellect and power, and she is virtually without equal.

Beyoncé is a beautiful woman who exudes raw sexuality while bowling us over with her tremendous talent. She causes not only conservatives, but some feminists, to cringe. The criticism seems to swirl around the idea that prominently displaying her breasts and shaking her booty diminishes women. Some might say, "Well, that's not classy." But she is a twenty-first-century entertainer, and in that respect, she is no different than a bygone-era actress. It is what lies beneath that entertaining exterior that defines classy in the most modern way.

If her booty was all there was to Beyoncé, critics might have a point. But her intelligence, along with her talent and drive, has brought about her achievements. She has enjoyed record-breaking career success and has taken control of a multimillion-dollar empire in a male-run industry, while being outspoken about gender bias and the sacrifices women are required to make.

In the February, 2013 issue of *GQ,* Beyoncé is quoted as saying, "Let's face it, money gives men the power to run the show. It gives men the power to define value. They define what's sexy. And men define what's feminine. It's ridiculous."

Note her tone of confidence, her intelligence and her articulation, which we've determined are all major components of class. Beyoncé is working on our behalf to level the playing field, and even beat men at their own game. Exhibiting her sexuality on a grand scale while she's playing a man's game does not diminish her. She is intelligent and powerful enough to do so, and no amount of stereotyping can diminish her essence.

A classy woman is subtle and understated. This is one of the most important qualities and distinguishing characteristic of having class. To be classy, you must be subtle in many areas of your life. Subtlety implies a degree of moderation. Have you ever been anywhere and noticed a woman who is flamboyant, and who tries to too hard to attract attention? Didn't you feel a slight amount of embarrassment for her?

A subtle woman has style but she doesn't look like a designer model. She dresses sexy but does not look trashy. She puts on such a small amount of perfume and make-up that one can barely tell that she has any. (Although men do appreciate a knock-out shade of lipstick that goes well with your coloring.)

She talks just enough, but certainly not too much. She

doesn't dominate a conversation, and she asks questions of others and listens to their answers. Her laughter is pleasant to hear but not too loud. She rarely swears, and her voice is soft and sensual. A classy woman will usually come across as "low-key" in a social situation. This is not to say that she is shy or lacking confidence. On the contrary, her confidence puts her at ease and relieves her of any desire or need to validate herself to those in her company.

A classy woman doesn't brag about her success and attributes. A woman who has true class and strong sense of self does not need to run around and tell everyone how smart and successful she is, whether it's in person, or on a social media site. This urge to validate yourself through bragging is a clear sign of insecurity, which will never be found in any definition of classy. A classy woman lets her actions, rather than her words, prove to others who she is, and she is not compelled to announce to everyone how special she is.

A classy woman responds to adversity with dignity. A classy woman knows how to get angry without losing her dignity. She doesn't get abusive or violent with men unless the circumstances really justify such an extreme response, like physical aggression. She knows that there is always the option of simply walking away from a bad situation.

I was once paired with a man at a dinner party. Though he was just average in looks, he exuded charm. When he asked me to have dinner that weekend, I accepted. I chose to meet him at the restaurant, for reasons that weren't entirely clear to me at the time. But my "instincts" had kicked in for a reason.

Before I continue with the story, I would like to emphasize that your instincts are important and valid, and should never be ignored. Don't dismiss them when they kick in. Never worry about feeling or looking foolish if you listen to, and act according to, your instincts. They are there to protect you; honor them.

While having dinner, he began to assess my appearance. "You know, you have beautiful hair, but why do you wear it in that style?" *What?!* My answer was as simple as, "Because it suits me." Moving on . . .

"You have such white teeth. They are almost perfect, but you have a tiny gap right here . . ." he said, pointing to his own mouth to show me where my imperfection lay. *Say what?!* No one had ever commented negatively on my teeth, and in fact, I often had been told I had a nice smile. Yet this average frump of a man was pointing out a flaw?

My response? A laugh and a reply, "Yes, I hounded my poor orthodontist to remove my braces, and I didn't torque them as long as I should have." I'm good natured and tend to give people the benefit of the doubt; and although I was taken aback, I wasn't really offended.

But then talk segued into his saying, "You are going to love my house."

"I beg your pardon?" I asked.

"Well, naturally, you'll want to come back to my house with me," he said with a smug smile.

Ah, now I saw where he was going with the subtle insults. He was trying to make me feel that I wasn't quite up to snuff, but I could make up for my "shortcomings" if I went back to his house and tried to show him just how much I needed his approval by having sex with him.

"I don't think so, no," I told him.

"Ah, we'll see. How about dessert first? A meal without dessert is like sex without an orgasm," he said. It was so obvious this was a worn-out line of his, and at that point in our acquaintance, he was way out of line.

I realized that I didn't want to spend one more moment with this man who sought to control how events between us unfolded. Yes, we were at dinner in an elegant restaurant, but that did not mean I had to stay.

I placed my napkin on the table, stood up, and said, "Excuse me, I'm leaving."

He said, "You can't just leave, that's rude!"

I looked him right in the eye and said in a low, measured, and assured tone, "You've cornered the market on rudeness this evening. Nothing I do could possibly top it." And I turned and walked out of the restaurant, head held high, hitting a natural an unhurried stride, without so much as a backward glance.

There was no scene, no screaming, no public displays of emotion. I just left. I showed my pride at an appropriate time. I wish I could say I had always acted with such dignity, but that was something I had to practice and learn.

Revisiting the importance of listening to your instincts: I listened to my instincts and drove myself to the restaurant that night. Would this controlling and manipulative man have taken me to my home, or—against my will—to his? What might have been the consequences if I had not listened to my instincts?

♀

How You Say What You Say

No matter what your look, it is what comes out of your mouth that most significantly defines your class and elegance.

Have you ever seen a woman who looked classy, based on the criteria I discussed here, but then she opens her mouth, and her façade was blown?

It is not just the words that are used; it is the voice used to deliver them that denote class. There is nothing more alluring about a woman than a cultured voice. You want to cultivate an attractive voice. Cultivate means the development or improvement of physical qualities by special training. Concerning your voice, it means learning the proper pronunciation of words, practiced articulation, and words delivered with poise, so that they flow.

Audrey Hepburn's voice was cultured and measured, her words eloquent and sure. Her womanliness and seductiveness seeped out through every syllable because she was practiced and confident in her delivery.

Marilyn Monroe's voice was breathy and almost little girlish, but she articulated each word as it flowed from her mouth. The fact that there was a whole lot of woman behind her voice made it seductive, as well.

A seductive voice is much more easily attained if the basics of a cultured voice are an integral part of your speech.

Women like Marilyn Monroe are routinely stereotyped; and while we can never slay stereotyping, we can deeply wound it when we apply ourselves to the task.

If you haven't seen it, I urge you to watch the movie, *Working Girl.* The two main characters in the movie, at first, seem miles apart in terms of class. Katherine is a Manhattan-ite from a privileged background who had the benefit of an Ivy League education. Tess is a Brooklyn working girl who went to night school to get her degree, but who has, as she put it, "a mind for business and a bod for sin."

What distinguishes Tess and has you rooting for her is her desire to constantly improve herself. She practices enunciation, for instance, in an attempt to rid herself of an accent that pigeonholes her.

Tess asks for Katherine's advice about how she dresses, and she listens and acts accordingly, because she recognizes what sets her apart from women like Katherine, whom she desires to be more like. She intuitively knows that classy, understated, but intelligent women are the ones who climb the corporate ladder and attract the best of men.

What Tess is really going for is subtlety. Subtlety implies a degree of moderation, a lack of flamboyance, and the lack of the impulse to attract attention. We meet Tess when she has a large mess of hair, too much eye makeup, and a clutter of jangly jewelry. Katherine, Tess's boss, is wearing a classic suit, has stylish hair, and dons understated jewelry. Katherine has style, but she doesn't look like a walking high-fashion advertisement. Her voice is soft but very sure, and she puts her points across without raising her voice or resorting to foul language. It's all about self-perceived power, and unless you learn to perceive yourself as having power, you won't be able to take the next steps that are necessary to set you apart as classy. The basics start with impeccable grooming and timeless fashion sense.

Being classy, however, does not mean being sexless. Just because you wear a subtle suit that doesn't emphasize every curve doesn't mean there isn't a lot of sexiness going on underneath those clothes. But you don't have to flaunt it, you don't have to try to grab attention, and you don't have to verbally remind someone of how sexual you are. The way you dress, speak, and carry yourself makes the first favorable impression, and it makes men want to know what lies beneath that cool and classy exterior.

Men may like the sleek design, the perfect paint job and the sophisticated styling of a Mercedes coupe, but they also want to know what's under the hood.

That is what you want to be—sleek and smooth, perfectly made up, and sophisticated, but with the promise of real horsepower underneath the exterior.

But you must have an exterior appearance that invites a man to peek underneath.

You know elegance when you see it, and so does a man. Elegance is telling in the manner in which a woman carries herself in every situation—whether walking into a family dinner or an extravagant party.

Elegance is displayed in voice, movement, manner of speech, the way you stand and sit, and the way you respond to those you come into contact with.

Some of these traits, such as your voice and your walk, are part of your nature, while other elements of elegance, such as your interpersonal skills, are undeniably linked to your upbringing. But as has been pointed out throughout this book, any and all of these qualities can be improved with practice. Many qualities are acquired through habit or from friends. The point is that class and elegance can be learned. Perhaps your family circumstances didn't foster these traits. But there are enough movies, photos, and even tutorials that can help you overcome any deficiencies in these areas. You just have to want to improve yourself. It is easily achievable if you watch, look and listen.

Observing women who are known to be classy and paying attention to their behavior and actions will take you a long way toward achieving your goal of elegant and classy. All it takes is a willingness to assimilate information and actually put it into play.

Again, fake it 'til you make it. Imitate actions that you perceive make someone classy (whether in the movies or in real life). Soon enough, that imitation will turn into your reality. Paying attention and trying to identify the specific elements of the behavior and actions that make certain women stand out and come across as more classy can take any woman who wants to become more classy a long way toward that goal.

When it comes to elegance and class, there is no such thing as small and insignificant. After all, being classy is a sum of many, many elements of a woman's personality, behavior, and actions—some of which are more obvious than others—but all of which are essential for the total package to be considered elegant and classy.

If you can incorporate some, many, or even all of these traits into your life, you will have a great start on your personal journey toward becoming a more attractive woman to everyone in every walk of life, and especially to the men you wish to attract into your life.

Have the courage, determination, and intelligence to go through that metamorphosis and you will enhance your womanly power.

CHAPTER FIVE

SIMPLE, EFFECTIVE WAYS TO IMPROVE YOUR ATTRACTIVENESS

The very most important thing you can do for yourself is to come to believe in your own attractiveness. I don't care who looks back at you in the mirror, you must come to feel that person is *as beautiful as she can be*. Few people in this world are born with beautiful faces and bodies; and even if we were, those things become more difficult to maintain as we get older.

But that really doesn't matter. What matters is that you make the most of what you have. When you are satisfied that you have taken proper steps to make the most of what you have, you will feel attractive. You know how you feel when you've just gotten a great haircut, or had a professional at the department store makeup counter do your makeup? You know the pleasure you have, the confidence you exude as you leave the salon or the store? Or when you are really decked out, and you get those coveted looks of admiration, doesn't your self-esteem soar? You can have that feeling all the time if you just follow a few basic rules.

Let's face it: There are certain physical basics in our society which just have to be observed. You are going to laugh at this one, yet it is something that many men over the years told me they really liked . . . *cleanliness.*

There is nothing that is more of a turn-off to a man than a woman who does not care enough about herself to follow a basic hygiene regimen.

Just think about how you would react to a man who isn't very hygienic. You want to be with a man who is freshly shaved (unless he wears a groomed beard) and showered. You want a man who wears clothes that haven't been thrown in the dryer to remove wrinkles, and even odors, before putting them on for the third time (for some men, warm equals clean!) You don't want to have to "get past" his two-day beard, grimy fingernails, unbrushed teeth, or visible nose hair before attempting intimacy. Mature and classy men hold women to certain high standards, just as you—as a classy and mature woman—should hold men to certain high standards.

One of the most frequent compliments I received from my sex partners was, "I love that you're so clean." And on no part of a woman's body is this more appreciated than having a clean vagina. For sex, especially oral sex, you absolutely must be clean. There are feminine hygiene cleansing products languishing on store shelves. Pick some up and use them, so that you are always prepared for intimacy.

I discussed this with a man who was just a great friend for many of those years I was single. We never had sex, but we talked about that and many other things. I was fortunate to have him in my life, because he gave me great perspectives, while validating or dispelling my thoughts about men.

I once asked him, "Why do men comment so often about how clean I am? Are there a lot of women who aren't clean?"

He responded, "Some aren't, especially down there. Sometimes you have to practically hold your nose when you go down on a woman."

Ewwwww!

Don't be that disgusting woman. Don't even put yourself in the position of thinking, *Do I smell okay?* as he heads south. When you are clean, you are confident. When you are confident, you are sexier. Clean and sexy go hand in hand. Good personal hygiene is *vital* to self-esteem.

Men notice your personal grooming more than you would ever expect them to. I had discussed this with the same male friend, but I also had a great opportunity to get some objective feedback from six men who were at the same out-of-town banking conference as I. One evening after dinner, we headed to the hotel lounge for an after-dinner drink. I've never been shy about asking direct questions of men, and I took advantage of our camaraderie and comfort with each other (no doubt lubricated by a few glasses of wine) to do just that.

I was the only woman in the group, and it was so much fun to be able to engage in this kind of conversation and to have these men share their thoughts and opinions. Over the years, I found (made) opportunities to ask other men about these issues, and the answers are almost 100 percent in accord with those I learned on that night spent talking and laughing with those six men.

One of the first things I asked was, "What physical things about a woman are turn offs?" The first—and to me, the most interesting remark one man made—was about the excess hair on a woman's body. All of the other men chimed in with, "Oh, yeah," or "Oh, no," so I said, "Tell me more!" And did they ever! The first thing to come up, surprisingly, was facial hair. They all agreed facial hair was totally gross on a woman. A mustache was bad enough, but chin hair really chilled them. They think, *Hey, you look in the mirror, how can you not see that?!*

"What about hair on other parts of women's body?" I asked.

"You mean like, is she too hairy?" one man responded.

"Yes. Is that an issue?" I asked.

That set off a hilarious but enlightening conversation. One

man talked about how he reached under a woman's dress to run his hand up her leg, and he felt like his hand had been stabbed. "She knew we were going to third base, and she didn't even shave her legs?" he intoned, shaking his head.

"Okay, what about the more personal areas?" I asked. This got a variety of answers, but there was general agreement that the amount of hair in that region didn't matter, as long as it was trimmed and everything was clean. This was before the Brazilian bikini wax sensation hit American women, so the topic of "totally bare" didn't come up. But since then, I have asked men about that as well. (Yes, I'm shameless, but you'd be surprised how willing men are to talk about the things that frustrate and flummox them about women. Besides, if I had not asked dozens of men over more than three decades about these things, I wouldn't be able to share them with you here.) Regarding "totally bare," a majority of men seem to like it, though it is not requisite by any means. But trimmed . . . trimmed is always requisite.

One hairy area that was mentioned, which I had never thought of, was the hair coming up from the pubic area onto the stomach. Men would prefer not to see that. And believe it or not, one man brought up nipple hair. "How does she get rid of that? I mean, that has to be painful," another man observed.

I thought about how painful the bikini waxes I had been getting for more than ten years at that time were, and said, "Speaking of painful, have any of you men ever been waxed down there?" They were incredulous, and the expected choruses of "No way!" and "Damn, that would hurt!" surfaced. I assured them it was indeed painful, and chided them about being wusses when it came to pain. They all laughed and readily admitted that was so.

I asked that same group of six men about hairy underarms,

and to a man, they all thought hairy underarms were a major turnoff. "This isn't Europe," one said.

Most often men notice a woman's head of hair. If it is dull and dirty looking, or if she has long-unattended dark roots, it is a signal to a man that you don't take proper care of the other parts of your body, either. If you can't be bothered to wash your hair before going to work or going out clubbing, he wonders what else you are neglecting. More comments about hair include color and styling, "Why does she still have those curly bangs?" "That hair down to her ass is ridiculous." "What's with hairspray? I hate the feel of hairspray." "The worst is when women dye their hair Crayola orange and blue. It is not natural. I know your boyfriend didn't tell you to do that!"

A woman's hands, especially her fingernails, are something else that men notice almost 100 percent of the time. Men like to see that a woman has painted and shaped nails, or at least nails that aren't bitten and ragged.

If you are wearing sandals that show off your feet, a man is going to take a look at your toenails. He may not care that they aren't particularly pretty feet, but toenails tell a tale in themselves. One man made a comment about getting "scratched up in bed," and although I laughed when he said it, he added, "That's something that can actually keep me from coming back for more."

Nice teeth seem to send a primordial signal to a man. Nice teeth denote health, and although a man may not be thinking as far ahead as good genes being passed on to his offspring, that intuitive thought is in his subconscious. "A great smile gets me every time," a number of men have told me. "She's gotta have fresh breath," others have said. Good dental hygiene promotes all kinds of good thoughts about you.

Finally, smooth skin gets a lot of thumbs up from men. Soft

skin is something they attribute to being ultra feminine. They love to run their hands over our smooth skin. Using moisturizers and lotions can keep your skin oh so touchable.

The impression of cleanliness also extends to your abode. The brother of a good friend of mine was great to talk to about men's thoughts on women. He was a really handsome man, in his mid-twenties, smart, funny and just so nice; so much so that if I'd had a little sister, I would have thrown her at him. One night I was having dinner with him and his sister—my friend—and he told us he had just stopped dating a woman because "she was dirty."

"What do you mean by dirty?" I asked. "Her, personally, or her apartment?"

"Both," he said, shaking his head. He talked about how when they first started dating, she always looked good. But after a few weeks, she started getting sloppy. "How was she sloppy?" I asked.

"It wasn't just her body, you know?" he began. "She'd let her dirty clothes pile up in a corner of her bedroom, and I swear she put things on that hadn't been washed. They had stains on them, and a couple of times I got a sour smell off of her. I wasn't even thinking about marrying her, but I thought about how she'd be with children. Would she let them go around in dirty clothes, too?" Interesting that a man would think that far, isn't it?

I once said to my ex brother-in-law, who was another great man to bounce things off of, "You know, men really expect a lot from women. Sometimes I think they're delusional. Women have to do so much more grooming than a man. It's time consuming and it's expensive, and sometimes painful. It just doesn't seem fair."

His response was, "A relationship or marriage is a partnership. Men and women alike need to do the necessary things to make sure their partner is pleased. Sometimes things seem unfair and I understand that. But to keep score and say we are delusional isn't the right way to look at it, in my opinion. Yes, we may want the world from our women, but then it's our job to make sure you're taken care of and appreciated for your efforts."

And there you have it—the reasons why you will always want to be at your best when it comes to hygiene and grooming. It is noticed, and it is appreciated.

CHAPTER SIX

FLIRTING

Okay, you've worked on enhancing your class, social skills, personal appearance, and hygiene. All of these improvements will put you in the position of confidently meeting men, while putting the full force of your feminine power in play. The man won't always come to you, so you may have to rely on that age-old, ever-effective art of flirting. Don't be afraid! It is so much fun!

You may have to overcome some inhibitions to be an effective flirt. There is an art to flirting, and it has everything to do with sexuality and confidence and nothing to do with actual sex—that comes later. For now, you're just trying to get that man interested in you.

Though this section of the book may sound a bit like an "instruction manual," these are tried and true methods of flirting, and they will very often get the desired response.

Again—and always—never forget that he's *just* a man. That's all there is to him. He wants what every woman has, and now the thing to do is to make him want what *you* have to offer, and the individual sexuality that is uniquely *yours*.

Okay, you've spotted an interesting man, and you want to get his attention.

A great smile goes a long way in flirting. This is a simple way to make a good first move.

Another fine way to get his attention is to shoot him a short, darting glance. He'll pick up that you're interested, and then when he comes your way, unleash that great smile.

You can also look straight at him and toss your hair, or sensually run your fingers through your hair. Not in a challenging way, just a *feminine way.* Practice this in front of your mirror so that it looks natural and sexy. And this is where cleanliness and good grooming come in. Have hair that is attractive enough to toss. It doesn't have to be long, you can toss short hair with your fingers and look sexy doing so. A second part of this is to look at him, toss your head (which causes your lovely clean hair to move seductively), and look back at him.

When you know he is looking at you, tilt your head and touch your exposed neck. Again, practice this in front of your mirror so that it comes off looking sensuous, not like you are scratching a mosquito bite.

Once you've gotten his attention, and you've made eye contact, lick your lips (again, practice in front of the mirror) then look away.

If the opportunity presents itself, brush up against the man. Be subtle, applying just a little pressure with only *one part* of your body. Your thigh rests against his for a long second. Your arm comes in contact with his arm for a brief moment. I don't recommend pressing your breasts into a stranger unless you are really looking to get laid. If that's your goal, press any part of your body against any of his with no guilt or embarrassment. However, if you are looking to start something more like a relationship, go slowly. A subtle form of contact would be brushing his hand as he hands you a drink or passes the bowl of mixed nuts. Touching is a powerful flirtation tool.

Any one of these flirtation tools lets a man know you are interested, and between his libido and his ego, there's a very good chance he's going to want to get to know you better.

Don't be hesitant about making the first move in any instance. You have a right to select and pursue even the finest-looking man in the room. And please, don't be shy about trying these things! With his ego, he will forget you made the first move, and he will forget he was naturally responding to your nonverbal yet sensuous advances. Remember *where* men operate from and believe in the power that gives you!

Taking Flirting to a Higher Level

Okay, you've got his attention, and he is by your side, whether you've walked up to him or he has made his way over to you. There are some crucial things you need to do to keep him there. *Speak.* A simple "hi" will do for starters. Or make a clever observation about something going on around you, something he can see as obviously as you can, giving him an opportunity to respond. Keep your tone light, almost like you have smile in your voice.

When he does respond, fully turn your head toward his. Don't be looking off into the distance because you are too shy to face him. If you fail to face him, you have made him feel you are not openly acknowledging what he said, and he might shy away from further comments and it's over before it could even get started.

Turning your head toward him and giving him your full attention leads to conversation. We've talked about how to make conversation, so put it to use here. Find something interesting about him and comment on it. ("I see you have the new Samsung Galaxy. I'm thinking about getting a new phone. How do you like it?") As the conversation progresses, turn your shoulders toward him, then your upper body, then finally your knees, so that you are now fully facing him. This should happen over the course of a couple of minutes. He *will* respond in kind.

This is a good time to try touching. Whether it is a result of passing the peanuts or whether you touch his arm with the tips of your fingers, you are making important contact. Make it light, almost imperceptible. His response to your touch will tell you whether this interlude is going anywhere or not. If he receives it well, and even returns it, then you are making a lot of progress.

Next, and this is a little tricky, but it gives him a "sign" that things are going well between you. Anticipate his movements. If he reaches for his drink, you reach for yours at the same time, almost bumping each other's hands. Laugh as if it were a mistake.

If he starts moving to some music, get in sync with his movements. Subtle, soft, but right on the same beat. If he notices this, again laugh as if it were such a fun coincidence.

If he turns his head to look at something, turn yours at the same time, observe what he is observing. When he looks back at you, you can give him any number of signs to let him know you saw what he saw in the same way he saw it. A smile, a nod, a tinge of amusement in your eyes, a slightly wide-open eye expression of "can you believe it?" Whatever the situation calls for, make him think you are on his wavelength. He will end up thinking how very much you two have in common. Again, this calls for being aware and looking for opportunities. It's really so easy, and you'll love the results!

With each practiced flirtation, even if you don't get the results you want, you are getting better and better at it. You will fail at times. You will come close to succeeding at times before the interlude disintegrates. But you will definitely succeed at times! Regardless, you are learning and growing and improving your flirtation skills, and you are growing more confident with each interlude.

And as a reminder, you were alone when you began the flirtation, so if it doesn't come to the point you had hoped for, if he says, "Well it's been nice talking to you, but I have to be somewhere," you are no worse off than when you began.

You tried, you stepped out of your comfort zone, so naturally you learned something and you have one more experience at flirting under your belt. These experiences are what help you mature into the woman you wish to be.

CHAPTER SEVEN

STRONG AND FEMININE

Webster's Dictionary defines strong as: *Physically powerful; muscular. In good or sound heath, robust. Capable of enduring stress or strain. Intense in degree or quality. Forceful or persuasive. Extreme, drastic.*

Webster defines feminine as: *Of or belonging to the female sex. Marked by qualities attributed to women.*

As you can see, strong and feminine are *not* contradictory terms. Nowhere does the definition of feminine say, "Weak, without muscles; in poor health, lethargic; incapable of enduring stress or strain; lack of intensity in degree or quality. Mealy-mouthed or non-persuasive."

Your femininity *is* your strength, and strength is absolutely an essential part of being a complete woman. Femininity is essential if you are going to be strong enough to grab hold of a man's heart.

Strength in the context of this book means being able to take someone's best shot (emotionally, not physically) pick yourself up, and go on with your life, all the while cloaked in confidence.

Feminine in the context of this book means using all your nature-given womanly wiles to their best advantage.

Important Uses of Strength

You must be strong in order to recognize the signs of, and

subsequently to deflect, emotional, verbal, and physical abuse. Your femininity won't stand for abuse of any kind. Any man who displays any symptoms of abuse is not worth one single moment of your time.

Emotional abuse is a serious problem, and you must recognize the signs and be willing to walk—no, *run*—at the first sign of it.

Trying to exert control over you is one of the most egregious of emotional abuses a man can be guilty of. If, at the beginning of a relationship, the man accelerates the pace of the relationship by talking about commitment, living together, or marriage, don't take this as a sign he is madly in love with you. Don't be fooled into thinking, "I've just met the perfect man because he wants *me*!" Slow down, and watch for other signs. He may be trying to reel you in so that he can gain control over you.

Does he question you about your past, wanting to know everything about you and your previous sex partners? *Danger!* If that word could be printed in red here, it might emphasize this point so you would never, ever forget it. You *do not* owe any man any explanations about, or descriptions of, your past sexual experiences. He might say he wants to know in order to get to know you better, to find out how good he is in comparison, to feel closer to you . . . any number of false reasons. What he will do with the information you give him is intimidate you, bully you, try to make you feel guilty, and humiliate you. And God help you if he ever gets in a position to do that. Don't let him.

If a man asks you anything about your past sexual experiences, your response *must be,* "That's none of your business." If he drops it right then and there, you can move forward in the relationship. He might next say, "Well, tell me about just one of your old boyfriends. Just *one*, come on." He is testing you. If he can get you to tell him about one relationship, then he knows he can "negotiate" with you. When you tell him, "That's none of your business," stick to it. *The point is not negotiable.* If he persists, *get out, get out, get out!* This is a man seeking control, and it is the first step to an unbalanced relationship. If he knows something about your past, and brings it up, you must respond, "Hey, if you don't like it, that's your problem. It's *my* past, and I'm living with it just fine." If he drops it, move forward. If he badgers you, get out!

I had a friend whose husband I did not particularly like for many reasons, but my dislike was amplified when he said to me one day, "I know how to make Debbie cry. I just throw her past lovers up to her." Is that control in its ugliest form, or what? Debbie gave him that control when she told him—at his insistence—about her past sexual partners. If she had just been strong enough to say, "That's none of your business," when he insisted, one of two things would have happened: He might have married her anyway, accepting the person she had become as a result of being the sum total of all of her life experiences, including sexual experiences; or, he might have left her because he felt too insecure to deal with someone he couldn't control. There is a third option, but you can't really even consider it an option. He might have married her anyway, and then worked on changing her and controlling her when it would be more difficult for her to walk away. If you use the tools given to you in this book, you will never find yourself in that position.

Control is not about love. It's about ego.

You must accept who you are—with all your past indiscrepancies and warts—because doing so gives you the power to basically tell a man to get lost if he doesn't like something that you *can't change* (your past) or *won't change* (things you like about yourself).

Another form of abuse which women often mistake for love is a man's unwillingness to share you—with your friends, your family, your co-workers. If he wants all of your time away from your work, he is again seeking to control you. If he gives you a hard time about it, if he tries to make you feel guilty, then you absolutely must say, "I'm going out with my friends after work, and if you don't like it, don't call me anymore."

There is only one appropriate response a man can give to you in either of these situations—acceptance.

You will find out how much he likes you in a hurry if you tell him, up front, *no*. No, I will not talk about my past. No, I will not make myself exclusively available to you. If he backs off, says he's sorry, and behaves normally, i.e., accepts what you have told him, then you've broken him of a habit he has previously used to control women. Good for you! If he doesn't back off and becomes even more possessive, you must break off the relationship immediately. Possessiveness does not equal love or even affection. Possessiveness is a very selfish trait. Again, it's about ego and control. You must be able to say no and *make him live with it*.

If that means he never brings up these issues again, you have been successful. If he says he can't live with your ultimatums, *tell him it is over*. Mean it. Don't put any conditions on it. Don't negotiate. He either accepts it or he doesn't.

If you are dating him and another man at the same time, you do not have to justify it or apologize for doing so. If you are truly enjoying dating more than one man and don't feel a desire to be in a monogamous relationship, then *that is your right*.

If a man wants to look at your phone, then he wants to look into your life; and since you don't know how he plans to use the information he sees there, you should never relinquish your phone. Do you really want to deal with his asking, "Who's

Tom?" It doesn't matter if Tom is your brother or your lover, it is none of his business until you choose to tell him about Tom, or anyone else in your life. This is also an issue of his respecting your privacy, and if he doesn't, you know his needs matter more to him than yours do.

If he says, "What are you hiding?" or anything along that line, it's a ploy to put you on the defensive. Don't let him. You have to be able to stand up for yourself and say, "I'm not hiding anything, but I value my privacy." The same goes for any area of your life you deem private. Your phone, your wallet, your drawers—these are things that are uniquely yours, and they are turned off or snapped closed or shut for a reason. If you ever catch him invading your privacy without your permission, you know you can never, ever trust him.

Some men think they have a right to pry into your life, but they are looking for information that they can use to control you. Why else do they seek knowledge that you haven't chosen to share?

There is one absolute, fail-proof thing you can say in any of these situations which draws a line in the sand and lets him know exactly where you stand and how he must *accept* your "no" and accept you for who you are. I call it the *Golden Door Rule.* If he says he doesn't like the fact that you slept with other men before him, that you have social interests outside of him, or if he tells you that you have to choose between him and another man when you don't want to be put in a position of choosing, then you *must* look him in the eye and say, *"If you don't like it, you know where the door is."*

This is a pivotal point in a relationship. If he walks out the door, count your blessings. These demands were only the beginning, and if you had given in on any point, you would have allowed him to get some degree of control over you.

And why should you give any man any control over you? Why make yourself powerless? For certain, you won't be happy. As children, we had to accept the control our parents had over us—they met our needs to survive. At work, we have to accept the control our boss has over us—a paycheck meets our current needs to survive. But with a man, well, he is *just* a man, and he is not entitled to any control in any aspect or in any measure in your life. Why add a negative factor to your life? A controlling man will not make your life any better, but he will absolutely make it worse—much worse.

Okay, so he leaves and now you are *alone* again. Whew! No one to control you! Doesn't the relief more than make up for being alone?

But if he stays, if he doesn't walk out the door, then you have put the relationship solidly in your court. You can completely control the game, and you are on your way to making him fall in love with you.

Remember, emotional strength plus femininity equals power.

CHAPTER EIGHT

HOW TO KNOW IF HE IS RIGHT FOR YOU

Once you've established your feminine power in your relationship and he is definitely interested in you and you're interested in him, you must ask yourself several questions. Whether you ask these questions before or after you have had sex, the answers will help you to either move forward or move away.

1) **Does he make you feel better about yourself when you are with him?**

By following the enhanced self-esteem suggestions made earlier in the book, it is a given that you already feel good about yourself. But do you feel *better* about yourself when you are with him? In other words, does he *enhance* your being?

There's one simple way to answer this question—when he leaves, whether at the end of a date or after sex—do you feel happy or do you feel depressed? There isn't much in between when you are at this point in a relationship. Has he complimented you, wooed you, and been attentive and kind to you? Or has he commented negatively on your thighs, made you do all the work during sex, or left without kind words or considerate gestures?

In the beginning of a relationship, if he isn't making you feel good about yourself, then you are wasting your time. If a relationship is ending, you might expect him to be unkind. But in the beginning? No. (Recall the story of the man who insulted me in the restaurant.) Where do you go from there, except straight downhill into relationship hell?

2) **Does he *consider you* in making decisions?**

It could be something as simple as what movie to see or what kind of food to eat. If he asks you and you say, "Oh, you pick," then he has considered you even if he ultimately makes the decision. But if he doesn't even bother to ask you, *then he lacks respect for you.* It's a simple as that.

You know the infinite importance of respect in a relationship, so you realize that if he doesn't even consider you, he will never respect you. If he doesn't care about your opinion enough to seek it on trivial matters, then what are the chances he will respect you on important issues, such as degree of commitment or how many children to have? No, if he doesn't consider you in decisions or choices, he is selfish and controlling, and we know what that means. He's out the door! Remember the Golden Door Rule: "I want to be consulted about decisions you make for us, and if you can't do that, then you know where the door is."

Don't use the Golden Door Rule casually. It should only be used when it comes to a control issue. You can't invoke the rule because he doesn't like the cat hair on your sofa. He has a right to be annoyed that you didn't bother to vacuum or use a roller on your furniture. This doesn't go to the core of who you are, it only addresses the need for you to be a little more aware of the comfort of invited guests.

Now if he says, "I hate cats and if this relationship is going to have any chance at all, you're going to have to get rid of it," then of course you would invoke the Golden Door Rule. That does go to the core of who you are—a cat lover.

Every time you use the Golden Door Rule effectively and correctly, you are strengthening your position in the relationship—

but you are also giving him a chance to reform. Maybe he has always made decisions, because the women he dated in the past liked it that way. Maybe some misguided, desperate woman gave away her cat when he gave her an ultimatum. Maybe he has always gotten answers to his queries about previous lovers. Maybe he has gotten his way when he made a woman choose between him and another man. That doesn't mean you have to let him continue that pattern. *You set the rules, he lives by them.* If he can't change, can't consider you, then you've lost nothing (if you didn't have his respect, you had nothing anyway). However, you will have gained something very important—more respect for *yourself.*

Each time you apply the Golden Door Rule, whatever the outcome, you win. Either he comes around, or you become stronger. *You win.*

3) Does he make you laugh?

This goes beyond being happy. Does his sense of humor connect with your sense of humor? Laughter is as essential an ingredient in a good relationship as beef is to beef stew. Laughter takes us beyond happy—it means we experience joy. Happy in a relationship means you smile when you think about him, that you are content with him, that you are comfortable and secure in your coupling.

Joy is the next level of happiness. Webster defines it as *a feeling of great pleasure or happiness.* Not just ordinarily happy, but extraordinarily happy. If you can't laugh, you can't experience joy. Joy "juices up" a relationship. It keeps it from drying up and withering away. So be sure you can laugh with this man, because through laughter you can experience great happiness and you have a much better chance at having a long-term relationship.

4) Does he excite you sexually?

I saved a very important point for last. Are you *in heat* over this man? Do you have luscious feelings when you think about him, touch him, kiss him? Does he get your juices flowing? Many women have been to bed with men with whom they feel only a slight attraction, or even no attraction. The women who do this, do it for many reasons. They might tell themselves, "It's better than nothing," or "If I don't have sex with him he'll stop seeing me," or "He really wants it, so I guess I'll do it."

Whatever.

And that's fine. Really, it is fine to have sex with a man for any reason, but it is only sex. But honestly, how much pleasure can you get out of sex if you go through the act without any strong *sexual* feelings toward the man? You don't have to love him, by any means. Heck, you don't even have to like him a whole lot. Men sleep with women all the time for no other reason than they want to have sex. They don't even consider whether they like them or not. You have every right to do the same thing. If he turns you on, then you have everything you need to power this relationship to the next level and far beyond, if you choose to go there.

CHAPTER NINE

THE GOOD STUFF

So you want to have sex with a certain man? You don't even have to wonder if he wants to have sex with you, because if you have been together for one hour or one year and *you* want to have sex with *him*, he is going to want to have sex with you. He's *just a* man.

Blow Jobs

I do not write this section lightly, because there are different schools of thought on this particular sex act, but I am giving you the benefit of my experience, and the experience of many women and men I've spoken to about this over the years.

If I were to lay down one sex rule here, I would say never, ever, definitely not ever, give a blow job on the first date.

Now "a date" can mean you met him in a bar, and you end up in the back seat of his car, or you go home together. It can also mean he called you up, made a date a week ago, came to your door with flowers, and took you to dinner.

Under either circumstance, or anything in between, *do not give him a blow job on your first date.*

I readily admit that my experience is "dated" in this regard, since a blow job is something that seems to have evolved over the years in terms of acceptance and utility. But the advice in this book, as we said at the beginning, is based upon not only my experience, and not only the experience of dozens of women and men I have talked with, but upon history of sex through the ages. Fundamentals that have applied through the years in terms of a woman wanting a man who respects her, have not changed. But sexually transmitted diseases and instantly available pornography have put a new spin on blow jobs.

You have been taught that intercourse can lead to sexually transmitted infections—but not necessarily that oral sex may, too. So it has become a "safe" way to satisfy a man. Men in their twenties and thirties now think, "Blow jobs are safe, you like me, do me."

What exactly are you getting out of that? Now, you may be a woman who is stimulated by giving blow jobs, and that is the reason you do it. Great, that's healthy sexuality. May I ask you to please hold off for a bit, however?

Do you do it because you think it is not as "intimate" as sex? *Au contraire*, if you'll pardon my French. There is another school of thought that says a blow job is the icing on the cake. A privilege he has to earn. After all, it is for him a real treat to lay back and watch a woman's head bob up and down as she labors (and face it, that's why it's called a "job") to bring him sexual gratification.

Do you do it because you think if you don't, he'll lose interest in you, and won't ask you out on a second date?

Let's look at it this way—*him first*. I have talked to dozens of men about giving oral sex, and it seems to be a fifty-fifty proposition. Some men absolutely love it, and when pressed as to why, it has to do with giving the woman satisfaction. It makes a man feel good to know that those moans, those hands fisted in the bed sheets, and of course an orgasm, are the results of something he is doing to her. These are giving men. They don't care how much hair you may or may not have down there. They are not particularly put off by natural odors—your body has different scents right before you start your period, when you have just come off your period, and when you are ovulating. These are actually aphrodisiacs to many men. However a neglected and unwashed vagina can be a big turnoff, and uncleanliness is the *main reason* men don't want to go down on a woman. He may have had a really bad experience with a woman's poor hygiene in the past.

If you are hygienic, and a man still has any problem with giving you oral pleasure, then he is a selfish man and everything that happens going forward will be built on his selfishness.

A blow job in the front seat of a car, with a guy you just met, or are on a first date with, is simply not the way to make the most of your feminine power. *And blow jobs do give you a certain measure of power.* As we saw in the *Urban Dictionary* definition of a woman, there was this: *"Highly attracted to males of the species who are reasonable to look at, have jobs, are relatively kind, sometimes take out trash, and treat them like equals (not superiors, not inferiors—equals.) Happily give blowjobs* (sic) *in return."*

Honestly, if a man does all of these things, he's the type of man who deserves a blow job! But you have to spend time with him to find out if he is indeed that kind of man. What do you know about him on a first date, after all?

It takes more than one date to determine if he does those things described above, and to determine that he believes in equality and is not just out to get satisfaction his way. But if he is just the opposite—boorish, unkind, entitled or misogynistic—the kind who pushes your head into his lap after the first kisses, then you are giving him something that *gives him power over you*.

When a man knows that you are *bestowing* a blow job upon

him, that gives you the power. If he really wants a blow job, he has to earn it.

And then there is just oral sex without ejaculation, which can be very satisfying for both of you as it segues into actual sex. You don't have to bring a man to climax in your mouth for fellatio to be enjoyable for him. You will find it more enjoyable also if you, like a number of women, don't like the taste of semen and don't allow it in your mouth.

I was with three male friends and asked them about this—did it occur to them that women might not like the taste of semen? One man said, "I figure if they swallow, they like it." Another man said, "There are two kinds—swallowers and spitters." The last man spoke up and said, "There's a third kind—dodgers!"

We had a good laugh about that, but you know what? You have every right to dodge that stream of semen. I asked the men if they minded when a woman spat or dodged. All three men in general said that when there is emotional involvement with a woman, they liked her to swallow because there was a romantic connection. But notice that they said it mattered when there was emotional involvement. Otherwise, it didn't really matter. You still got him to the point of ejaculation . . . he's happy.

♀

Sex, Sex, Sex

The first and foremost thing about having sex with a man is to make him think *he* seduced *you*. I don't care if you have thrown yourself at him, ripped his clothes off, and mounted him, it is important for him to believe he was stud enough to make you want to do it.

But you, *in making the most of your womanly power,* will be more in control of how his emotions will flow.

Let's talk about the seduction and actions leading up to sex. First, you have to have some righteous kissing. This might happen on the first or second date, or it might happen fifteen minutes after you've met him. Sensuous, warm, tingling kissing. Even if he isn't a great kisser, let him know *you* are. Some basics on being a great kisser include a soft, receptive mouth. If he is cramming his tongue down your throat, gently push him back, withdraw, then take the initiative and *kiss him* the way you want to kiss. You might have to do this more than once. It's kind of like training a puppy, it takes patience and persistence, but he will eventually catch on. The most important thing for you to do is to let your sexual feelings guide your kissing. Mmm, kissing, mmm sex, mmm yummy! It should not be practiced or mechanical, but responsive from the deepest part of your womanliness.

So relax, let your juices flow, and let those natural, womanly feelings be the basis of your kissing. Great kissing is such an aphrodisiac for a man.

Then there comes the body contact. Nothing like ever-so-slightly pressing your breasts into his chest, then gently, almost imperceptibly, shifting them while pressing the tiniest bit more firmly into his chest. You will get more excited, as will be evidenced by your taut nipples, and he will undeniably, indisputably, become more excited by the powerful sexuality he feels coming off of you.

Now, *stop.* You need to catch your breath. He will come at you again immediately, but you will stop him by putting your hand on his chest. You will take a deep breath, look away, and either flip or finger your hair, as if you are trying to cool down. Then you will look back at him, directly into his eyes—and he will be watching you intently—and that look will tell him that you can't resist him, so that when he comes at you again, you moan softly and appear to be giving in to his tremendous seductive powers.

Oh darling, you've begun the conquest!

♀

When Is the Time Right for Sex?

When is the time right? Anytime you feel secure enough to handle the outcome, the time is right. What do I mean by outcome? Let's look at post-coital emotions.

Whether sex was fabulous and you've fallen in love with this sex machine, or it was terrible and you can't wait for him to get off of you, you have to be secure enough to deal with those feelings. You also have to be secure enough to handle *his* feelings. He may have just had the greatest sex of his life and fallen madly in lust with you, or he hated it and can't wait to get away from you. Either way, there's a lot of complexity to the aftermath of first-time sex, and you need to be strong enough to handle it and act properly, either way.

Let's talk about one-night stands, because if you can understand what a man thinks in this regard, you will be better able to handle whatever occurs. Being prepared to deal with it will ease tensions and smooth the way for better sex, no matter what the outcome.

A one-night stand can be an emotionally difficult experience for a woman. A one-night stand for a woman with a man she is actually interested in, and hoping to have a relationship with, can be very disappointing. Meeting an attractive, interesting guy, going out with him, liking him, and ending up sleeping with him only to never hear from him again afterwards often feels like a debasement and an utter waste of time. I encourage you to change your thinking in this regard. Just like each time you take a chance on talking to a stranger, you have had an experience to learn from, and the same is true even if what you hoped would be more, turns into just a one-night stand.

This is something I heard often from women, and like most things, the experience is incredibly similar in each instance. It generally goes like this: "We went out, and he seemed to be really into me. He was all over me, and we spent an incredible night together. He told me that he really liked me and that he couldn't wait to see me again, but I haven't heard from him since. Why did he do that? I thought he really liked me as much as I liked him, and I thought it would be more than a one-night stand."

Slapdash statistics seem to bear out the fact that just because a guy has sex with you, that doesn't mean that he finds you particularly attractive or that he perceives you as girlfriend material. Unlike most women, men can have one-night stands with women for whom they don't really have much attraction.

It is possible that he does like you, but it's also possible that he doesn't have anything better going on at the time, and you are just a mildly interesting person he dates, and has sex with, while he is looking for someone who he really wants to be with. As unkind and as selfish as that sounds, it's quite common for guys to look for sex and one-night stands, and to do and say whatever it takes to find a sex partner and temporary female companionship just for fun. In actuality, he might be looking for a more serious partner, or he might be taking a break from anything resembling a relationship.

Just because a guy you are out with is making out with you and is all over you, does not mean that he finds you very attractive or particularly sexy. This sounds totally contrary to what you have intuited about men, but you might be attractive and sexy enough for him at that very moment to satisfy his sexual drive and need for physical contact. This is especially true if he hasn't had sex in a while or if he just broke up with someone and is looking for female company to assuage his bruised feelings. This doesn't mean that he finds you beautiful, or that he would like to have any kind of relationship with you.

Though this is a tough reality to accept, but for your own emotional health, you should learn to do so.

Men have told me that they don't have to particularly like a woman to find her sexually attractive. A man may have a sexual appetite that needs to be sated, and that could be with any woman he doesn't find physically repulsive. Yes, those are pretty low standards, but he is, after all, just a man.

Men are base in that regard, as they don't always have the highest standards when it comes to satisfying their sexual needs. In general, women are not as loose about standards, though there is nothing wrong with it if she is. A man who is sexually starving will likely find physical pleasure and satisfaction from having sex with any woman who is not repulsive to him. He will be looking for that single, one-time physical satisfaction from that encounter with a woman, but he will want nothing more from her in the future.

A typical woman might be justifiably misled by a guy's affectionate behavior towards her when they start seeing each other, believing that his touching her is a sign of possibly genuine care and a long-term interest, but more often or not, this sensuality is just an attempt to escalate the interaction toward a one-night stand, which for him is a one-time sexual experience and nothing more.

This is why it is important for you to begin to think like a man about sex. There is no rule that says only men can experience a pleasurable sexual experience or an ego boost from a one-night stand. Women can do the same, because they can put themselves in the same place emotionally as a man . . . attracted enough to want to have sex, but not attracted enough to want a relationship. You can look at it like he's filling in until you find someone you really want to be with.

Men often look at a one-night stand as a "victory," because it validates their self-esteem. You can do the same, without apology. You're entitled to enjoy sex for sex's sake, without putting any expectations on it.

Sometimes men themselves don't know why they have one night stands. They might be blinded by lust to the degree where they honestly don't know what they want until after they satisfy their sexual urges. A man who thinks that he is interested in dating a certain woman might change his mind immediately after having sex with her, realizing that he wants nothing else from her than what he just received, a one-night stand, but he might not necessarily have planned to be with you specifically. It just happened.

Take that same approach! If you don't experiment with different sexual partners and satisfy your own needs, you are denying yourself pleasurable experiences while you sit home and wait for Mr. Right to show up at your door.

The more sexual experiences you have, the better lover you become, the more you can discern if a man is a good lover, and most of all, you give off sexual vibes that are infinitely more attractive.

Men sense a sexual woman—going back to the pheromones—and they will seek you out for sex, and a possible relationship, much more readily than they will a woman who guards her sex and sexuality like treasures in a castle.

If you can learn the difference between something and everything, i.e., an enjoyable sexual encounter versus a proposal of marriage, you will become more powerful. Your womanliness is deeply tied to your sexuality, and when you use your sexuality for your own gratification, you are in control.

Some one-night stands can be exciting adventures which will leave great impressions, while others might make you feel used and slightly depressed. You can avoid those negative feelings if you approach a one-night stand as an experience into which you enter with no expectation of anything but an enjoyable sexual interlude. If you have no expectations, you can have no disappointments.

If you are with a man and it becomes obvious that you are going to have sex, get into the frame of mind that it is *something you are choosing to do*, and therefore you have control. This is most beneficial because, when you are not pinning any hopes on it being anything other than just a single sexual encounter, you can be more relaxed and even more turned on. Because nothing is riding on the act itself, or what comes after, you are more uninhibited and free to just enjoy the experience.

CHAPTER TEN

SEX SCENARIOS

In this chapter, you will learn about the four most common post-sex scenarios you can expect the first time you have sex with a new partner. Knowing the proper way to handle each scenario will enhance your self-esteem and lead to awareness and growth in conscious thought.

Scenario #1: This man was a fabulous lover—oh, wow, you knew you were attracted to him, but now you think you could be in love with him! How can you be cool, and not scare him off?

Scenario #2: What a disappointment! He was selfish, unskilled, sweated too much, talked too much, had too much body hair, failed to please you. Any one of these things or more can make for bad sex. You don't want him near you again. How can you break it off cleanly?

Scenario #3: You thought he was okay, but he thought you were unbelievably great. What's the next step?

Scenario #4: He can't wait to leave, and you can tell he'll never call again, it was that bad. How to keep your dignity as he walks out on you?

In the next chapter, we discuss how to make sure you get better and better at sex, so that by the time you finish this book, I don't expect Scenario #4 to be a viable option, but it has happened to enough women that it is a possibility.

♀

Scenario # 1
Sex was great! You could fall in love!

Scene: He was a fabulous lover and now you have definitely fallen for him. Tread lightly, ladies. That doesn't mean that you can't tell him what a fabulous lover he was—in fact, you should. But you also have to take this moment in time to throw him completely off balance so that you don't seem too anxious and send him running out the door.

Here's how. Do not, and I mean *do not,* ask him to stay. You are an actress playing a role, if that's how you must think of it, but you have to seem simply satisfied, not enamored. This is an extremely important point for the next round of action in the game. Keep the ball in your court. Even if you are in a daze from great lovemaking, keep your head.

Certainly, you may feel that all you want is to have him wrap you in his arms and never let go—at least not for the night. Feeling as you do, you might say, "That was so wonderful, I feel so close to you right now that I want you to stay here and hold me all night." In a perfect world, a man would melt at those words. Well, we live in an imperfect world, so 99 times out of 100, he will want to run! There is always that wonderful exception when you both feel that way, and falling asleep in each other's arms is natural.

But you cannot make that happen by entreating him to stay. Even if he was thinking about staying, you've just scared the hell out of him. He will have any number of excuses ready to use to get away, because he will feel pressured.

Men despise feeling pressured. It's that control issue again, but it's true. Even if he was having warm feelings about you and anticipating seeing you again, you have just reduced the chances that he will do that. So take the strong position and say, "That was really great, but you don't have to stay." Now take the womanly position and sexily roll away from him with a satisfied sigh, and let him make the next move. Don't put any play into these words. Say them with warmth, wrapped in slight disinterest. Your body will be angled away from his, or you will be looking at the ceiling. Stay there. This will make him crazy! Why? Because you are controlling the situation. A man's ego can't take that kind of nonchalance, especially when he knows how much you enjoyed yourself.

If he says, "But I'd like to stay," remain nonchalant. I always advise women to seem sweet while they are saying things that cut a man to the quick. Your sexy-voice response would be, "Mmm, fine, but I do have to get up early in the morning." Don't say why you have to get up early. Don't answer him if he asks why. The most you will give him in the way of an answer is, "I just have to be up early." Then set (or check) the alarm.

Now he's really getting anxious. This is where you have to keep the man working *for you*. He should be slightly unsure and experience a bit of anxiety. Remember, you have what he wants and he has to work to get it. If you have sex again during the night, terrific! It has already been established he is staying until morning.

Now, it's morning and the alarm goes off. You are sure you are in love now. So what do you do?

Hustle him off, quickly but nicely. This is when your vulnerability is most likely to show itself, and he doesn't want to see that. So, continuing your performance, you will say, "This has been nice, but you really have to go now." A quick kiss, a moment of endearment, whatever—but then you are out of that bed and you are handing him his clothes. Notice I said handing them to him, not tossing them at him. You are being polite, a good hostess, but the good hostessing stops there.

Do not fix him breakfast. Do not even offer him a cup of

coffee. You have to be somewhere—remember? You are busy. Just because you had great sex, your life is not revolving around this man. *That is the message you must give him if you want him to come back, panting for more.*

What have you learned about men? You've learned they don't like needy, clinging women. They don't like to be pressured. They don't like to talk about their feelings. Look how accommodating you are being. You haven't made him do one thing he doesn't like. That in itself makes you more desirable, but the fact that you are "kicking him out" makes him insecure, and the more insecure he is, the more he reaches out for security and assurance. Instead of running from you, he'll be reaching for you!

See where we are going here? Sure you do. Make him feel insecure and unsure and you become more attractive to him.

Isn't this what men do to women all the time? So why can't we do it and have fun doing it? It is the most liberating experience you can have in dating—turning the tables on a man. You've established even more power. And how did you do that? Your feminine wiles reeled him in, and your strength gave you the courage to throw him back—at least for now. Don't worry. He'll take the bait next time, too.

♀

Scenario #2
Sex was, if not horrible, a real disappointment.

I have had enough experience to know that if he isn't a decent lover the first time, he isn't going to improve with practice. You must assume he's had practice before he found you, yet he's still clueless, which means he's either selfish or he has a really slow learning curve.

That is not going to change with time or frequency. If the sex is bad, the relationship is already doomed, so why prolong it? There are reasons to do so, such as he loves to travel first class to wonderful places and wants to take you with him. If you seek adventure and can tolerate bad sex as a trade-off, then that's a good reason to keep him around. Eventually the bad sex will overshadow the Champs-Élysées and you'll end the relationship.

But if he is just a man who won't be taking you any further than the restaurant on the corner, ditch him. You have to do it quickly, and in this case, without intentional pain. Don't cause unnecessary pain, but don't let anything—pity, guilt, politeness—keep you from doing what you have to do to end it right there.

Sex is over, and now you know, so is any chance of a relationship. It was bad sex. You do not have to lie, make excuses, let him down easy, or be coy. Think . . . what would a man do? (Besides lie and say he'll call you.) Try this on for size:

"Well, I have to get up early in the morning, so you better go."

Chances are he knows you didn't enjoy it, so his ego will be hurt. He'll look for solace. Do not give it to him.

"Wasn't sex good for you?"

"Frankly, no."

"Why not?"

"Bill, it's either good or it's not. You know that. I don't have to explain."

"It will get better."

"I don't see that it will. I've enjoyed knowing you, but you really have to leave now."

Don't say, "Maybe you're right." Don't say, "Well, give me a call sometime and we'll see." Just end it. In this case, you *can* toss the bad lover his clothes.

This sounds rather harsh, doesn't it? But it isn't really; it just goes against the convention that women should "let a guy down easy." Women are taught to be kind and nurturing and soothing, and being abrupt goes against what we have learned. But anything less than abrupt in this situation will only lead to having to say goodbye again later, when you have had more bad sex and it is even harder to extract the man from your life.

♀

Scenario #3:
It was just okay for you, but he loved it!

Later in this book, you will learn how to be a fantastic lover. It doesn't require anything extraneous, no *Kama Sutra* positions or fancy accoutrements. When that becomes the case, Scenario #3 is the most likely to happen to you.

Consider that it was merely okay for you, but he loved it. He is trainable. He will be willing and anxious to please you in order to keep getting enjoyable sex. Never be afraid to tell a man anything about what makes you feel good, or, alternatively, what turns you off. It's your body and your right to have the best sex you can have. So if this happens, of course he will be back, and you can gently guide him to all the right spots, and away from all the wrong ones.

If he continues to do things that turn you off (licking your forehead like a dog, tickling you with his tongue under your armpit, nibbling at your areola instead of giving you the hard suck you need, or any number of bad habits he picked up along the way) then you just have to tell him outright, "That does nothing for me, please don't do it anymore."

His response might be, "No one's ever complained before."

Many men use this line whether it is true or not. You can't blame them, their ego is bruised. Now give it another bruise by saying (in that sweet voice) "Obviously those women haven't had as many good lovers as I have or they would know the difference." Ouch. He may be temporarily miffed, but he will rise to the challenge you have just given him—to come up to par with your other good lovers. I have said this to men deliberately to bring them down a peg. It works every single time. Not even the most egotistical lover is secure enough to hear himself compared unfavorably with your other lovers. It's a really good tool to use with men who think they are the world's gift to women. Now he'll listen and try hard to please you.

I was once dating a man who got into a weight-loss and exercise routine that whittled his masculine physique down to toothpick status. I was lying in bed, watching him dress, and I said, "Your thighs are too thin now." (We women can get away with insulting a man's thighs. He's not nearly as invested in their appearance as we are.)

His response was, "I don't care if you like them or not, I like being this thin."

My response? "Fine. Fortunately I have other lovers who have sexy, masculine thighs."

Do you think this will make a man run out the door? Think again. You sometimes just have to do the verbal equivalent of shanking a man to bring him to his knees.

This particular man gained some weight, and later asked me to marry him.

Women who understand this about men expect a man to take the pain and then apologize for his inadequacies.

Here's a wonderful little story that embodies this concept:

A man was napping on the sofa when his three-year-old daughter stabbed him with a sharp pencil. Surprised and in pain, he sat up and yelled, "What did you do that for?!" The little girl began to cry, and the father reached for her and soothed her and apologized for yelling at her.

His wife stood in the doorway, watching this interaction with pride. Her daughter had already learned how to hurt and man and make him apologize.

If you think this is a novel concept, it is not. If you think it is cruel, consider it from another point of view. It is an observable fact that is written about in literature and talked about in movies. It is something that some women know intuitively, and other women can learn.

Consider this concept of "hurting a man and making him apologize," as another version of "men love bitches."

Keeping a man off balance and flattening his ego, when justified, are tools you will want to learn to use to keep the power in the relationship balanced, and even in your favor.

It is really fun to do, and it allows you to say what's really on your mind. If you do compare him to other men for any reason, and he says, "Well, what did they do/have that I didn't?" you are being put in a situation—intentionally or unintentionally—where you are again being asked to disclose your past, and you do not want to do that. Your response should be, "Every man is different. I'll show you what I like." Period. Never, ever let a man put you on the defensive. That's where you should be keeping him until he proves you no longer need to do so.

Scenario #4
He can't wait to get out the door.

This happens, and it can be devastating. I had two friends to whom this seemed to happen more often than it should. We talked it through, and we realized that under most circumstances, the sex had not been good for her. If it wasn't good for her, there were two reasons: She wasn't a good enough lover, or he was a selfish lover.

If you think it might be because you were not a good lover, acknowledge that. It is important to acknowledge that you need to improve as a lover, just as you would improve with practice in any physical activity.

Take tennis as an example. You look good in that tennis outfit/you look good in that pencil skirt. You walk onto the tennis court with confidence/you walk into an event with confidence. You hit a few practice balls with your partner/you practice your flirting skills. You bounce the ball, preparing to serve/you move closer, brushing his hand. You serve into the net/you get no response to your touch. You fail to return a serve/you fail to get his full attention.

But each and every time you practice, you get better. The most important thing you can do to get better is to gain confidence with each failure. Does that sound at odds? Well who hasn't tried and failed and gotten better as a result? Whether it is an author who couldn't get her first or even fifth book published until she became a better writer, or whether it is a woman who can't get a man interested in her until she becomes a better seductress (flirt) it all comes down to practice, and learning from failure.

The whole point of this book is to help you gain confidence as you navigate the minefields of discovering your talents and improving until you, as a sex partner, are the equivalent of a professional tennis player. And it is not just about technique. It is about getting the feel for it. The rhythm, the confidence that comes with every good serve/with every successful seduction.

So let's get back to "fake it 'til you make it."

The best thing you can have going for you is your willingness to humiliate yourself, and still walk away knowing that the next time will be better.

Until you get better at sex, and know with certainty that is not your lack of sexuality that is causing him to bolt, you can assume he is a selfish lover. He got what he wanted, and he doesn't need to invest one more moment in you. This is more about him than it is about you. The only thing you can do to lessen the devastation is act with dignity. Never, ever, ask him to stay when he's obviously anxious to leave.

No matter how he lets you know it, you will know the sex was not good for him. Do not apologize. Do not try to justify anything ("I was just nervous," "It's been a while," etc.) Maintain your dignity. Do not in any way grovel. Don't demean him, either. The moment he rolls out of bed and starts looking for his pants, get up, put on a pretty robe, and go to the bathroom to give him a chance to get dressed without having to speak. Here's your chance to act with class and dignity, and even though you may never see him again, he will go away with a favorable impression of you. Why does that matter? Because every interlude you experience in your life should begin and end in a favorable manner. You never know if or when it will pay off, but you will feel better about yourself, which is an integral part of loving yourself.

If he starts to offer any kind of explanation or excuse for leaving, you can either let him explain or you can let him off the hook. The result is the same—he's leaving. You might say, "There's no need to discuss this. It just didn't work out. You take care of yourself." Then hold the door open for him. If he is looking at you, give him a little goodbye smile and/or wave. Then close the door. That's it. Simple, clean, dignified. Yes, it can be painful, but you will survive. And you will get better at sex.

The most important thing to remember in post-coital relations is this: Sex does not equal commitment. Even *great* sex does not mean a commitment is imminent. That's something you are going to have to come to grips with. I've had lovers who couldn't believe the sex they just had was so good. Many of my lovers said, "That's the best sex I've ever had," or "You're the best lover I've ever had." Not just one or two or even five men— many said it. But not one of them proposed *at that moment*. They may be awestruck, but men are skittish creatures and they don't trust those great feelings. They have to sort them out. What great sex does is keep the man coming back again and again until he doesn't want to go anywhere else for anything.

CHAPTER ELEVEN

BECOMING A GREAT LOVER

If you are a great lover, then your chances of having a man become more interested in pursuing you increase exponentially. I used to believe you were either a good lover or not, almost as if you were born with it. In any respect, it helps to have a developed and healthy sexuality. By healthy, I mean responsive and sure, assertive yet yielding to the magnificent feelings that having sex can elicit.

Over the years, however, as I coached girlfriends, (verbally, of course) I learned that healthy sexuality *can* be learned. But as with anything learned, it takes practice.

First, if you have never had an orgasm, then you simply must learn what one feels like. Masturbating can certainly get you there, but if you are uncomfortable or unpracticed with masturbating, I would strongly recommend buying a "neck massager." This is a wand-type instrument, with a large round rubber head, that you might find at Sharper Image. Or walk into a store that sells sex toys, and take the time to read what each one does. There is no need to be embarrassed. These places stay in business because many people walk through their doors looking for an instrument of sexual gratification.

Whatever you choose, use it to stimulate your clitoris to the point of orgasm. It's a safe and simple way to get the *feel* of an orgasm. Practice. As you begin having orgasms, be aware of the changes in your body, what you start feeling as you get close to climax. Don't worry that this will spoil you for men. Apples and oranges, literally. You are priming your body for orgasm. You are becoming aware of the pings that precede your orgasm. You become attuned to your body. Then, when you are having sex, you can start reaching for those feelings, instead of waiting for him to get you there on his own.

Orgasms can be elicited from various regions of the body, including the clitoris, vagina, G-spot, cervix, nipples, breasts, and anus. Studies have shown that up to 80 percent of women have difficulty achieving a vaginal orgasm, and indeed, if the clitoris is not stimulated during sex, then your ability to achieve an orgasm is diminished.

The right angle during sex can maximize the potential for clitoral stimulation. No special skills are required to achieve this. But during the act, if your clitoris is making contact with his pelvic area, you will be getting the double pleasure of clitoral stimulation and vaginal penetration, which can lead to the very pleasurable *blended orgasm*—both the clitoris and G-spot are involved in the orgasm.

Many women can only orgasm when they are on top. One of the things that make an orgasm easier to achieve when you are on top is stimulation, both internally and externally, which can bring on this blended orgasm.

But you can certainly achieve an orgasm in the missionary position. When he enters you, have him scoot up until his body is flat up against yours. With your legs at a forty-five degree angle, your hips are tilting upward. When you start moving together, direct the motion so that it is an up-and-down motion— steady rocking or grinding. Oh, there is immeasurable pleasure in a hard in and out thrust, but it is not the optimal action for achieving orgasm. To achieve orgasm, the focus should be on your clitoris hitting the base of his penis. You are pelvis-to-pelvis, rather than just in-and-out. Maintaining that pelvis-to-pelvis position keeps your clitoris in a position to be stimulated.

Any thrusting motion should be against your body, and the body part you want to be stimulated by that motion is your clitoris. You can also have him hold still while you rotate your hips to increase friction until you find your hot spot. The base of his penis should maintain constant contact with the clitoris, while the shaft and head of the penis massage the G-spot from the inside of your upward-tilted pelvis.

With him behind you, your body can easily be positioned so that your clitoris is making contact with the base of his penis, and you are again in a position to rotate your hips until you find your G-spot. Don't be afraid to reposition your body at any time during sex to maximize the contact. Feel your body's response to the position you are in, and allow it to seek out gratification.

And as we discussed earlier in the book, don't be afraid to let him know if he needs to move in a certain way to accommodate you. Try non-verbal communication first, and if he doesn't get the message, *tell him what you want.*

You've learned by masturbating or using a sex toy which angle works best and which part of your clitoris is most sensitive. *Go for it* in achieving that same stimulation from contact with your partner's body.

The only thing that would hold you back from an orgasm at that point is your mind—and the mind plays a very important part in your orgasm. If you have interrupting thoughts about whether or not you are performing well enough, or if you wonder if you are clean enough, or if your breasts are too small, or whether your roommate is going to walk in on you, then you are going to shut down your body's natural path to orgasm.

When you are having sex, you should be *in the moment,* with your thoughts solely concentrated on the feelings that are coursing through your body. *Feel it*, don't think about it. Sometimes *not* thinking too much is exactly what your mind needs. It will naturally, biologically, make the connections for you.

Your body, when responding naturally, is the most stimulating thing a man can experience. Your ardor incites him, and he performs better. When he performs better, your pleasure heightens. All of your other concerns are pointless, and are to him nonexistent, because he is going for his own orgasm, and if he can bring you along with him, so much the better.

Once you become aware of your body, you will recognize what you need to reach an orgasm. It might require your shifting your weight or body position, especially if your clitoris and your vagina are positioned farther apart than what is optimal. But you overcome such hindrances by reaching for that orgasm with your mind as well. Once you know how your body is supposed to feel, you can engineer positions and events to make that happen.

As you feel the buildup of pleasurable body sensations, allow your body and mind to *expect* an orgasm to follow. Keep all channels in your mind and body open as the excitement peaks with intensity. You will feel changes in your breathing, a feeling of warmth, sweating, body vibrations, altered consciousness, or an urge to moan or cry out. As you achieve an orgasm, notice the feelings you have all over your body, not just in that specific area. Sexual energy flows through you. Don't try to stop that flow in any way. Let your body and mind take you where it will. During orgasm, endorphins are released into the bloodstream and make you feel any combination of happy, flushed, warm, deeply relaxed, or even sleepy.

Then comes the extra bonus of multiple orgasms. You've read them in romance novels, and you may think, *That's ridiculous! This is fiction. How can these women have multiple orgasms?*

Here's how: You are already in a state of heightened sensuality. As you begin to come down from your orgasm, don't allow yourself to totally relax. Let those feelings that are making you feel so amazing continue to flow, and then reach for another orgasm while your body is still primed with endorphins. Position your body to stimulate your clitoris again, continue the thrusting motion—and even if he has already had an orgasm, keep him there, squeeze down tight on his penis, and *go for it in your mind.*

Once you have accomplished a second orgasm, there's a chance for a third, or even fourth, if the man has the stamina. Once you've learned to achieve a second orgasm, your body and mind remember what brought you to it, and they will cooperate with you in making it happen from that point on when you are having sex.

Another positive that comes from achieving even a single orgasm is increased confidence in your own sexuality. You know that you are capable of having an orgasm, and from that point on, you will expect to have at least one.

Because you know what you are capable of, you will be able to determine if a man is a good or bad lover, or somewhere in between. If you know you have the capacity to orgasm even once, then you know that any man who cannot help you achieve that is *lacking* in the lover department. In one study, 85 percent of men reported that their partner had an orgasm. However, only 64 percent of their female partners reported experiencing an orgasm, creating what some sexologists call an "orgasm gap."

With this disparity, it is obvious women fake orgasm. Sometimes it is to please a man, to make him feel more powerful, more virile. Other times, a woman just wants the bad sex to be over even as the man seems intent on continuing to try to bring her to orgasm.

I personally have never faked an orgasm, because if a man

couldn't bring orgasmic-me to that point, it was *his* problem. I had sex with a man whom I thought would be a good lover, but he was a terrible lover. He was sufficiently large, but he had no technique, and there was no chemistry. He just went on and on, without orgasming himself, and finally I said something about the duration. He said, "Yeah, I'm a real thoroughbred." No, I thought to myself, what he was, was a real plow horse. I actually had to bite my tongue to keep from saying those words. He thought his ability to last a very long time was a positive thing, but the problem was he had no talent, so his prolonged performance was just annoying.

But you can still enjoy sex even if he is not a particularly great lover. To do so, you should not worry about the man. He is there for you to use as a substitute for the sex toy that brought you to orgasm. One thing you can be sure of: *if you are enjoying yourself, he will be enjoying himself. If you are feeling really good, he is feeling really good.*

So often women seem to think they need to do fancy tricks to make a man happy in bed. The only trick you need to learn is how to please yourself. When a man knows a woman is feeling pleasure, he gets on board and goes along for that fantastic ride.

And that ride can take you both to magical places together.

The Beginning of a Relationship

It is my sincere desire that the information you have received in this book has given you insight into your womanly power, and the confidence to put that womanly power to its best use in finding a man with whom you can have a relationship.

Great sex, which you have learned to give and get by now,

smoothes the path to the beginnings of a relationship.

Relationships involve escalated emotions and uncertainty about how to act upon those emotions. They involve spending more time with each other so that you can learn more about each other. And they present the possibility of love.

All that you have learned here in *Book I: Making the Most of your Womanly Power* will also come into play in a relationship. But there are many more areas to be explored regarding your womanly power once you enter into a relationship.

In *Book II* of *He's Just A Man*, you'll learn how to navigate through relationships so that you have strong, sure footing. *Book II* will also guide you in using your womanly power to ensure that the relationship is not only a happy one, but a healthy one.

You'll be given the tools you need to achieve equality in all the ways that matter in a relationship, while maintaining your womanly power so that you always have the upper hand.

You will learn about the pitfalls of relationships and the things to look out for that might endanger the development of a happy and healthy union.

Book II includes love-and-relationship columns I wrote, because the great majority of letters I received were about the issues that crop up in every relationship. You'll be surprised how many of the issues and feelings that you're dealing with are the same ones many other women experience. So often, someone would read one of my columns and write me to say, "That column could have been about me!"

This just underscores the old idiom that the more things change, the more they stay the same. Modern-day trappings put a different façade on relationships, but underneath, the same elements that have brought men and women together for eons, and kept them together, are still in play today.

The one thing you can always count on, however, is that he is *just* a man, and because he is, he is defenseless against your womanly power.

Now get out there and start using it!

ACKNOWLEDGEMENTS

To all the people, both women and men, who have been so open and honest in discussing love, relationships, and of course, sex with me over these many years, so that we could all come to the point where we pursued love and relationships with more confidence. Many of you are still in my life, and I love all of you. Thank you to my girlfriends for your friendship and support in my writing endeavors, and for all the fun we had over the years in learning about how to make the most of our womanly power. And we did.

Thanks so much for reading HE'S JUST A MAN! I do hope you enjoyed it, and that you found the content to be useful and valuable and informative. If so, then I am extremely happy, because that was my intent in writing the book.

I would *very much appreciate* your leaving a review:

http://www.amazon.com/dp/B011SDRW0S

Please visit my website at www.rebeccajwarner.com to follow my blog that addresses your questions about relationships, and provides information and updates for Book 2 of HE'S JUST A MAN which discusses the ups and downs, ins and outs, and highs and lows of relationships.

Please visit and like my Rebecca Warner Author Facebook page at http://www.facebook.com/AuthorRebeccaWarner

And follow me on Twitter https://twitter.com/rjiltonwarner

And check out my fun and sassy Pinterest page for HE'S JUST A MAN at:
http://www.pinterest.com/rebeccaljwarner/hes-just-a-man

Made in the USA
Monee, IL
05 March 2023